PRODUCE YOURSELF!
Stand Up! Step Up! & Move!

A Dancer's View on Focus, Presence, and Confidence

by

Ann Marie DeAngelo

BALBOA
PRESS
A DIVISION OF HAY HOUSE

Balboa Press books may be ordered through booksellers or by contacting:

Balboa Press
A Division of Hay House
1663 Liberty Drive
Bloomington, IN 47403
www.balboapress.com
1 (877) 407-4847

Because of the dynamic nature of the Internet, any web addresses or links contained in this book may have changed since publication and may no longer be valid. The views expressed in this work are solely those of the author and do not necessarily reflect the views of the publisher, and the publisher hereby disclaims any responsibility for them.

The author of this book does not dispense medical advice or prescribe the use of any technique as a form of treatment for physical, emotional, or medical problems without the advice of a physician, either directly or indirectly. The intent of the author is only to offer information of a general nature to help you in your quest for emotional and spiritual well-being. In the event you use any of the information in this book for yourself, which is your constitutional right, the author and the publisher assume no responsibility for your actions.

Any people depicted in stock imagery provided by Thinkstock are models, and such images are being used for illustrative purposes only.
Certain stock imagery © Thinkstock.

Illustrations by Cynthia Gregory.

Scripture taken from the King James Version of the Bible.

Print information available on the last page.

ISBN: 978-1-5043-2501-1 (sc)
ISBN: 978-1-5043-2502-8 (e)

Balboa Press rev. date: 8/17/2015

Dedication

This work is dedicated to all dancers everywhere in all genres for their commitment to the art of dance—the tools without which choreographers would not be able to write/create or directors produce. And to my mother, who was the embodiment of positivity, despite all odds.

Foreword

Sometimes it seems like magic, but I've come to understand that there is a subtle yet substantial design for making extraordinary things happen. And Ann Marie De Angelo is an exemplar and guide in revealing the template of how to manifest the remarkable, whether performing on stage, directing a dance company, or in one's personal life.

Ann Marie had the vision to move beyond barriers in her mind to do the impossible on stage, which is reflected in her dance reviews as a performer who is "sensational" and "phenomenal." This vision translated further with her ability to dissolve obstacles in the dance world at large in a range of astonishing ways from cross-pollinating talents in different dance genres before it was popular, to performing and choreographing in Cuba, to working cross-culturally in Mexico. And reinventing the Joffrey Ballet in a new environment when she was associate director.

As an accomplished dancer, choreographer, and artistic director, she has immersed her life in understanding the creative force that engages when expansive thought becomes grounded in the body. This process of making creativity manifest takes an inspiration and gives it shape and form. Nothing becomes something; thought becomes movement in space and time; vision becomes accomplishment.

Pascal stated, "We know the truth not only by reason, but by heart." But it goes further than that: We manifest truth through *the body*. Ann Marie's unique contribution comes in translating the creative power of dance for transforming organizations and individual lives.

Tapping into the inner power that becomes a dazzling leap across the stage or rotating en pointe longer than seems humanly possible, is not only accessible to the artist. We all carry the potential to connect to creativity and direct it into areas of our life. Are we ready to increase our ability to manifest our goals and dreams? Ann Marie offers us a rare look into the intricate workings of forging creative new paths, with clear steps for transforming our lives.

—Leslie Davenport
Author of *Healing and Transformation through Self Guided Imagery*

Introduction: Growing Younger Thru Dance

The moment burns a hole in my memory still. While taking morning class in the Joffrey Ballet, sharing the unspoken language of dance and sweat with my peers, time stopped and I marveled: Why do ballet dancers seem ageless? Is it the daily physical exercise? Their positive attitude toward life? The commitment to the body and movement? Or is it the reverence required to succumb to the dance itself, expanding each moment so that we experience a kind of transcendence in consciousness? I concluded that I had no idea. *Dancer animals we are, a breed apart by far.* Years later, when I was associate director of the company and was teaching a ballet class, I was struck by the same perception. The age range was teens to mid-forties, yet it was impossible to tell the dancers' ages. As the class progressed, I noticed energies getting lighter and the joy of youth at play. Finally I had my answer: I concluded that dancers' youthfulness comes from a concentrated effort to elevate one's thoughts through the ritual of movement.

The dance or movement is not an antidote for living longer, but rather a necessary part of feeding our souls and keeping our spirits fresh and alive.

Dancers produce themselves. These shapers of light transcend time as they make their imagination visual. Consistent action conquers the mind, and a child-like wonder dispels negativity. Of course, the grace and ease we see on stage is only acquired through great discipline and practice. Dancers are athletes with an unwavering commitment to their art. They are focused. In a world of cell phones, internet, and social media, our attention is splintered. We are overwhelmed with too much information. We lose focus and our intentions get muddled, directions become unclear, and our confidence to make decisions wavers. We may appear to be present, but most of us live in the future (in our minds), colored by the past (what happened), while the present (now) eludes us and disappears the moment we tweet (I don't tweet!) We may live in the future, but we don't necessarily see one. And the scariest thing for anyone is to not see a future.

Dance Steps as Life Metaphor

This book is a series of stories accompanied by steps as metaphors, each of which embodies tools for manifesting, for showing us how to direct our movements on the inside so as to create specific results in our outer lives. My interview with myself at the beginning of this book reveals some of the experiences that offer insights into my journey from dancer to choreographer to director and producer. My message is twofold: move beyond the struggle of the mind into vision (beyond thought into feeling), and the concept "commit to completion" that leads to the birth of confidence. In my experience, the difference between success and near-success is confidence. A dancer's process is a spiritual act first and then a physical one. This book provides some insight into my process, a dancer's process.

Thought can only manifest when grounded in the body.

"We risked everything! We threw away our traditions—no one helped us, and there were no rules. We worked when there was No interest, No pattern, No precedent, No chance. And here we are today."

—Lynn Cohen, paraphrasing Agnes de Mille in *Broadway & Beyond* benefit for Career Transition For Dancers, 2013

Photo by Richard Termine

TABLE OF CONTENTS

PROLOGUE: Living Outside the Box 1

HOW TO USE THIS BOOK 14

Stand Up! (Be still)
    STEP ONE: Finding Center 15
    Feeling Presence
    STEP TWO: The Dancer's Stand 19
    Concentration and Focus
    STEP THREE: Plié. 26
    Commitment
    STEP FOUR: Relevé. 32
    Clarity
    STEP FIVE: Tendu. 40
    Connection
    STEP SIX: Port de Bras 47
    Coordinating a Plan
    STEP SEVEN: Positions 54
    Courage

Step Up! (Be connected)
    STEP EIGHT: Rehearsal Practice 62
    Consistency

Move! (Be in action)
    STEP NINE: The Performance and Bow 68
    Confidence and Completion
    THE NEXT STEP: Glissade 78
    Transition Steps

DANCERISMS: Thirty-One Days of Movement 85

About the Author 138

We Are Imagination in Motion

PROLOGUE: Living Outside the Box
An Interview with Myself

Photo by Herb Migdol, me in *Viva Vivaldi*

Grand Jeté

Grand Jeté (to jump): This ballet move requires the dancer to levitate their body up into the air: it's a spiritual act first, then a physical one. Dancers move beyond the mind, jumping over the thought that they can't, for example, fly through space. What thought can you leap over right now in order to move from what seems impossible, to what is possible?

MOVE! Get Out of Your Own Way

I contemplated having a well-known journalist interview me for this segment—but so often with artists, the questions can lead to unanticipated or controversial answers. Even a question about my favorite color would probably find me grasping after a "better" answer like, "Yes, I do believe the arts can save the planet!" Therefore, I decided that the best person to conduct this interview would be me, because I would know exactly the right questions to ask. So here we go!

Me: Someone recently said to you, "You defy conventional categorization," meaning it as a compliment. Is that true?

DeAngelo: Yes—and I didn't get the job!

Me: Oh, dear. Well, you've always been ahead of your time. What exactly does that *feel* like?

DeAngelo: That's a good question: reminds me of when I was interviewed for Time magazine years ago.

Me: Really? How so?

DeAngelo: Well, I began to recognize that negative projections from others really have nothing to do with me. At 5'1", many directors told me that I was too short to dance in their company. Robert Joffrey told me that three times. In fact, he said that he'd never use me in his company because I was too short.

Me: He used the word "never"?

DeAngelo: Yes, never. Obviously I proved him wrong by later becoming a star in his "all-star, no-star" system.

Me: And of course, by being interviewed by *Time* when you finally were in the company.

DeAngelo: Exactly. The article was about me being one of the most "promising ballerinas in America." The first thing the interviewer asked was, "So tell me, what does it *feel* like to be short?"

Me: And you said?

DeAngelo: I never *felt* short.

Lesson: Do not let others place limitations or false projections on you.

Me:　　　OK then! Let's go back to your beginning. Where did you start?

DeAngelo: It's not where you start, but where you finish.

Me:　　　Isn't that a song?

DeAngelo: Yes, a significant one for Tommy Tune.

Me:　　　Tommy Tune is 6'6": I wonder if he feels too tall? So what about the song?

DeAngelo: He sang it in a show called *Seesaw*. In 2008 I had the opportunity to work with him when he received the Rolex Award at one of the Career Transition for Dancers (CTFD) galas that I direct and produce each year. He wanted to do a "false start" before accepting his award—pretending that the number hadn't been rehearsed, so he'd have to quickly run through it in front of the audience before doing the real performance. My production team and I were afraid to risk it without a *real* rehearsal with the orchestra and talent. So I sought out D. J. Giagni (a Tony nominee and on the artistic team) who had long worked in the business. He was riding his motorcycle in Los Angeles when I called, and he said, "Tommy Tune is the *ONLY* one who can pull that off!" And Tommy did, brilliantly.

Thought: Risk is energizing. Any risk requires trust, courage, and abandon.

Me:　　　And the point is?

DeAngelo: I'm not sure.

Me:　　　Alright then, where did you finish?

DeAngelo: I'm not finished. I mean, we're always in process—even up to the end. Some of us have a hard time starting things; others have a hard time completing. Until, of course, we discover the essence of completion.

Me:　　　What do you mean?

DeAngelo: Completion is ongoing. The end is another beginning. So commit to completion! That's the basic concept of this book.

Concept: Focus inward on your intention while seeing the end result realized. Then see further...

Me: I don't get it.

DeAngelo: Many of us struggle with completing something. Dancers, on the other hand, devote their whole selves to their art. Commitment and completion are inherent in finishing a dance step, a class, a rehearsal, or a performance. "Commit to completion" is essentially a concept about action, about seeing the end result and then *beyond* it, enabling you to *act as if.* Once you see that you've already done it, it is easier to do it and be done with it. I think the technique for creating what we want is still not fully understood.

Me: Got it. Let's go back to your journey. What about some of the in between times?

DeAngelo: I wrote a show called *The Last of the Best* about her. She was "The Fabulous Miss N. B. Tween," a struggling quasi-entertainer modeled after every female icon. She was the only illegitimate daughter of the Statue of Liberty, which created confusion in her life. So she vacillated between living in the world of her head and the real world, until she met self-help guru Dr. Fig.

Said Miss Tween: "You know, sometimes I feel like I'm living my life, only I'm not a part of it. I mean, once I get to where I've been striving so hard to have gotten to, I realize that in the process of getting there, I've totally forgotten where I'd hoped to have originally gotten to in the first place—and I don't even notice that I got there when I do, because I'm already planning to get somewhere else! So where am I?"

Photo Ballet D'Angelo, of Julie Whitaker and Fabel

Me: I can relate to that, actually. It's like when you're too busy or too overwhelmed to notice that you've lost sight of your intent! Was the show a success?

DeAngelo: One reviewer thought so: "Expect the unexpected...pure entertainment, varied, colorful, upbeat...best described as an off-beat musical comedy."

4

Me: Sounds like Dr. Fig was a Dr. Phil.

DeAngelo: Oh, he was way before Dr. Phil! Dr. Fig taught the FIG Principle, a self-help idea. F. I. G.: Feel It Given, Face It Going, Focus It Gotten. When you get an idea, direct it somewhere specific and then see that you already have what you want. My mother loved this. She owned positivity. "Where there's a will, there's a way," she'd say. "Go to the mountain, or draw it to you. Either way, you have to move!"

Me: Ah! A dancer's way, perhaps?

DeAngelo: Maybe. Ballet dancers have an elevated perspective; they must, or they'd fall down. They experience creativity-through-the-body, a variety of different languages of feelings that move. They *allow* and *do* simultaneously, conquering our greatest challenge: the mind. Dancers experience stillness in movement and then move that stillness in space. They *visceralize.* Creators and doers—they oscillate between the unseen and seen. These instruments of the dance remind us that we, too, are instruments for our own creative expression.

Me: For me dancers are *awe-inspiring.* They *stop time*!

DeAngelo: I'd say they *expand* time by moving inward. In stillness they find movement.

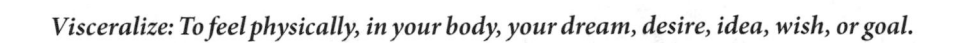

Visceralize: To feel physically, in your body, your dream, desire, idea, wish, or goal.

Me: You've been working in the dance world your entire life, moving seamlessly from one part of the field to another. When did you start studying ballet?

Me: I was three years old and cried a lot, so my mother worried that I wouldn't be able to integrate in school—or stop crying— and so she enrolled me in a local dance studio in Burbank, California. It was called "Roland and Reid Dance Studio." On cue, I cried in my first class, but she kept me enrolled anyway. Years later I thought of her vision when my big

Photo of me at age three

break came at the Joffrey. A fellow dancer broke his leg, and choreographer Gerald Arpino asked me to do his part. It was a virtuoso duel for two men in the fourth movement of a ballet called *Viva Vivaldi*. And it led to my first review mention.

"Miss DeAngelo, a small dancer with a high extension, strong technique, fabulous leaps and a manner reminiscent of Maya Plisetskaya, was the sensation of the evening."

—Anna Kisselgoff, *New York Times*

Fact: Persistence and determination alone are omnipotent.

Me: I never saw that ballet; or the one in which they say you hopped *en pointe* across the stage, like you are in this photo, where you're holding your foot in your hand.

DeAngelo: Yes, it was in the role of the Sun in Arpino's *The Relativity of Icarus*. That experience taught me to reach beyond the obvious. Arpino gave me courage to imagine the impossible. Fast-forward to 1995 when the Joffrey collapsed and he brought me to Chicago as his associate director—I gave him the courage to see beyond the collapse to the possibility of the company reviving. What goes around comes around.

Photo by Herb Migdol

"Ann Marie DeAngelo, a most spectacular dancer who never fails to dazzle, opened the ballet in a highly virtuosic solo that exploited her phenomenal technique."

—Anna Kisselgoff, *New York Times*

"The phenomenal Ann Marie DeAngelo as the dazzling Sun is sensational. She is wiry and perfectly proportioned...her leaps are glides and she whirls through pirouettes that an older dancer knows are impossible."

—Ann Barzel, *Chicago Sun Times*

Strive to do the impossible anyway.

Me:　　Other choreographers?

DeAngelo: I worked and performed with true innovators and pioneers: the voices that furthered dance, including Ashton, Balanchine, Cranko, DeMille, Fokine, Jooss, Kylian, Massine, Robbins, and Tudor. I later joined the Frankfurt Ballet in the mid-'80s when William Forsythe—who I knew from Joffrey II—first became director. But I broke my foot and ended up only being able to dance in an experimental German-expressionist piece by Christof Nels.

Injury is death for an athlete, but a setback can also be a positive impetus for change.

Me:　　Did you work with Twyla Tharp?

DeAngelo: The first time was in a ballet in the Joffrey called *As Time Goes By*. She was controversial then, and the senior members of the company refused to work with her, so all of the new apprentices got to be in her piece. She invented phrases like "the worm line," where fragmented steps became vocabulary. Later we were rehearsing a solo from another piece with lots of tricky weight shifts, and she asked me to do it with my eyes closed, laughing as I stumbled through. I learned that by closing my eyes my mind relaxed and I could see more clearly. The next step came more easily. I learned trust.

Me:　　Really? You learned all that from just moving with your eyes closed?

DeAngelo: Yes, try it! Close your eyes and take a step. First you might smile because of the unknown and then you will *feel* who you are. Some people are afraid to do just close their eyes an feel. Trusting others is trusting yourself!

Me:　　Let's segue to Varna, Bulgaria, in 1976.

DeAngelo: That was the year I went to the prestigious ballet competition held there. It was documented for Channel 11: now that was *real* reality TV. Same success formula as today: back-story and competition. I was the one they followed, and so naturally I got caught in a bit of drama.

After performing a solo from Alvin Ailey's *The River* (Alvin, a fan, gave me permission to perform it) I ran off stage kicking and screaming. Then I ran back onstage bowing gracefully to a cheering audience. That sequence repeated several times, and the camera caught it all. The downside is that it was shown in the documentary. The upside was meeting Alicia Alonso (a judge) who invited me to perform at her International Dance Festival in Cuba, beginning a twenty-year relationship with the National Ballet of Cuba.

Lesson: Put yourself out there and see who or what shows up. Connections are key.

Me: When did you first go to Cuba, which was then off-limits for Americans?

DeAngelo: That same year: I took Lawrence Rhodes, now director of Juilliard Dance, as my partner. Although there were no political relations back then, we had permission to participate in Alicia Alonso's festival because it was a cultural exchange. On the way down we got detained in Jamaica due to a terrorist attack. I was upset, not because of the potential danger but for missing rehearsals the next day. A few years later, Alonso asked me to bring a company of American works, including *Midler Medley*, and Ballet D'Angelo was launched.

Me: Yes, I remember that.

DeAngelo: Really? Were you there?

Me: No, I just read a review.

"Ann Marie DeAngelo turns out to be a surprisingly experimental choreographer. She brought great excitement to the International Ballet Festival in Havana with the creation of her work *Midler Medley*. In this ballet DeAngelo combines elements of classical ballet with her own vocabulary of natural human movement. Through superb usage of acrobatic technique, she penetrates a world of shattering solitude that is strung together through the prose of what Bette Midler sings. DeAngelo and her dancers point to what could well be converted into a new dance language; a classically oriented technique that accepts atmospheres, attitudes, expressions of film and musical comedy, and the happening of contemporary theatre.

—Alberto Dalal, *Revistas de Revista*, 1984

DeAngelo: From there a producer in Greece saw us and I hooked him up with another from Germany. Ballet D'Angelo toured Europe with edgy shows featuring an American pop sensibility. It was the start of my experimentation with blending styles, exploring audience accessibility and format, and the cross-pollination of talents. The Diaghilev/Fokine format (ballet-intermission-ballet), which was the status quo at that time, felt obsolete to me. My no-intermission, seventy-minute shows were called *Zeitgeist*, which means "spirit of the times." Diversity was organic, not preordained. I discovered that in bringing together opposites, there is sameness.

Me: Sounds very *now*.

DeAngelo: Indeed. The full-evening works had soul. Art as entertainment.

Me: What was your role in the Ballet de Monterrey (BdM)?

DeAngelo: I was the founding artistic director. It was funded by patron philanthropist and cultural aficionado Yolanda Santos Garza. Yolanda and I first met at her apartment on the Upper East Side in New York City. Next thing I knew, I was at a formal lunch with her and her family, surrounded by a vast collection of contemporary art. There I discovered the work of surrealist painter Alejandro Colunga, who I later commissioned for *Paradise*.

Me: Tell me more about *Paradise*.

DeAngelo: *Paradise* was a 45-minute piece based on the Adam and Eve mythos and set to the music of Yanni. I'd first created a segment of it for The National Ballet of Cuba, with the young and brilliantly talented ballerina Lorena Feijoo as the Serpent (she's now with San Francisco Ballet.) Yanni was originally going to play the ballet live, which is why I'd chosen pieces he'd orchestrated. But he was right on the brink of fame: he got his first big tour so he couldn't perform it. The last thing he said to me before creating the work was, "Close your eyes and imagine the silence before the curtain lifts—magic stirs. Start there."

Creativity: The alchemy of magic is transmuting energy into light.

Me: You've said that the serpent is an archetype of our time: why?

DeAngelo: I meant it in a Joseph Campbell sense. In other words, we are empowered by our own passion—serpent energy—to create. That's where our power lies, as well as in choice.

Me: What do you mean?

DeAngelo: Let me rephrase that: the *only* power we have is in choice. There is no mystery to life—we are here to create, be it babies or ballets. On tour with BdM in Guadalajara, a woman came up to me after a show and said she knew what my ballet was about: *Woman is Power and Power is Light.* I was surprised she understood that the essence of the piece was about "intuition." I still remember her wise old face.

Me: As you were cross-pollinating cross-culturally in Mexico, what was your greatest challenge?

DeAngelo: Aside from not speaking Spanish, some insecurity about creating a high-quality company, because ballet was not indigenous to their culture. But that quickly changed, and a great adventure followed. It was an exciting time, bringing together three cultures: Mexico, Cuba, and United States. Alonso's exchange gave me dancers, teachers, and ballet masters every season. I brought talents from the U.S.—and in the spirit of NAFTA, we also brought stage managers and lighting and scenic designers to train Mexicans in the various production areas.

Me: Pioneering!

DeAngelo: Yes. Even trusting Mr. Wiggles, an unknown element, was risky. Hip-hop was yet to be born, let alone accepted as a dance form. Back then, they hadn't even figured out how to teach their form, and there were no hip-hop classes.

Me: How did you discover Mr. Wiggles?

DeAngelo: I met him though his dance partner, Fable, who performed with Ballet D'Angelo. At that time these "street dancers" were not trusting of us or each other, for fear we'd steal steps from them or "bite their moves," as they'd say. My first rehearsal with Wiggles was in New York at Broadway Dance Center. We created a mime dance in his dance language set to a poem that served as the prologue to the ballet. He was later integrated in the piece as one thread, working alongside the highly-skilled Cuban ballet dancers and my muses. Then as now, I was marrying the past to the future.

In the beginning of Time
in a place in the Sky
there was a Light
It created Woman and Man
They were split apart
by a Serpent
This created conflict
and the Light disappeared
In the darkness sat the Unknown
waiting…
Now it is time to find the Light
again

Photo Ballet de Monterrey, Lorena Feijoo,
Mr. Wiggles, Ann Marie DeAngelo, Jesus Corrales
Front row: Abel Matus, Roberto Almaguer

"As a choreographer, she's way ahead of her time. She does story ballet in pure movement. You get the essence of the plot through what you feel. It's extraordinary."
—Melissa Hayden, *Dance Magazine*, 11/19/1992

Dancers allow and do simultaneously, conquering our greatest challenge—the mind.

Me: Following Ballet de Monterrey you were a part of relocating the Joffrey to Chicago, and worked for them thereafter. Did you continue to work on your aesthetic of a show that would amalgamate American dance genres?

DeAngelo: Yes, that was an ongoing quest from *The Variety Show—Jugglin' Styles* with composer and percussionist Marty Beller, Mr. Wiggles, and juggler/illusionist Michael Moschen as show threads. It included several diverse pieces such as Joanna Haigood's "Dance for Yal" performed by Jodie Gates and a mix of other artists. That was followed by *In The Mix!* and currently *America Dances!*

Me: You mentioned the concept of "art as entertainment."

DeAngelo: Well, on the one hand it's all entertainment, isn't it? Yet the arts are seminal to all other forms of entertainment—and vital to the growth of our culture. Here's the deal: you know the difference between something that lives in your memory forever (art) versus something that is enjoyable but forgettable.

Me: So what is your book really about?

DeAngelo: Perhaps it's not a book but rather a guide, or at best an oracle, and my take on what that is. Mostly it's about nothing.

Me: Nothing?

DeAngelo: In the creative darkness lives nothing. Nothing is so full of all possibility. Thank god for nothing!

Defy Categorization!

Photo by Richard Termine of *Industrial Rhythm*

HOW TO USE THIS BOOK

When you read the following stories, let the exercises serve as a guide in an area of your life that might be in need of movement or change. You may or may not choose to try them, especially the physical exercises. For dancers it might be for refining your process; for the dancer at heart it might be something to use as principals or tools in your lives. Play with the ideas and see if anything might resonate. *Stand Up!* offers stories and exercises geared to foster a world of inner awareness—your inscape. By putting the focus on your body, you become self-empowered in the same way that dancers do. *Step Up!* offers a practical application for grounding what you envision. It is the organization part of our process: the details, the plan. *Move!* is a message of how to move in the world from a place of authentic power, with courage and confidence. It is the performance, the pitch. The exercises in MOVE! Get Out of Your Own Way are there for the purpose of leaning about where to place your Focus. Is your Focus on you, on your intent/ objective, on a plan of action or on the result. Some of them have links to the the exercise online. Sometimes all that is necessary is to remember how to dream and act on that. More than anything, empowering yourself is key.

If something is missing in your life, it is most likely you!

14

STEP ONE: Finding Center
Feeling Presence

Photo by Martha Swope, Melissa Hayden in *Firebird*

In the Wings

I was nine years old and one of several students chosen to be a firefly in the New York City Ballet's production of *A Midsummer's Night Dream*. Standing offstage in the wings at the Greek Theater in Los Angeles, waiting for my musical cue to go on stage, I was awestruck at performing with a real professional ballet company. Entering before me was the ballerina, and as she swept by me I could feel her energy penetrate my skin. She walked out onto the stage with great authority and command. When she hit her mark, right smack in the center of the stage, she just stood there. She was alone, peering out into the darkness, in front of a vast audience. When I first heard the thunderous applause, I thought that it might be a riot or something. I was surprised that the audience was going so wild when she hadn't even started her dance. Weird. Time stopped again, and in that timeless moment I noticed how elegantly she received the recognition—she expected it, delighted in the attention—in this energetic exchange of love. I remember that moment more than her dancing. It was magical because the exchange that was communicated in that expanded moment was unspoken. I felt her radiance all the way over in the wings as her power magnified. She owned the world. She was Melissa Hayden, and it was my first taste of the commanding power of presence.

What is presence, that unseen charismatic aura? Dancers' presence is directly connected to the confidence they possess and exude, making them larger than life. We can all expand this quality of success that lives inside us.

Be the star you are! Your presence presents an idea.

Expanding with Presence: Magnetize
Take Hold of Your Power

Melissa Hayden showed me that the commanding power of presence is something that we can tangibly see and feel. Her confidence came from inside. She once said to me in a coaching session, "You don't love yourself enough." Years later she offered my dancers in Mexico the same advice. In order to be authentically confident, we must feel good about ourselves. When we feel good about ourselves and magnetize that feeling into an aura of belief, we become attractive and so draw things to us. In the same way, we can magnetize our goals and bring presence to them, whether it's earning more money or losing weight. When we become positive about taking action on one goal, others will follow suit. This requires belief and real trust. Hope is wanting but not really trusting that what you want is possible. Belief is *knowing* it is possible.

Going Within
Feeling Presence—Presence Yourself—Presence an Idea

Inner Smile: Close your eyes and smile quietly to yourself. Think about someone you like and imagine them smiling back at you. Imagine others smiling at you, complimenting you for what you are wearing or a job well done. Bask in the love others feel toward you, and in return, radiate back to them your own love.

Magnetizing: Amp up the feeling you just experienced, and imagine a golden glow of light surrounding you, an egg of light. Let it grow and get larger, filling the entire room with warm healing light. Feel the radiance of *you.*

Imaging: Expanding farther, imagine a person or goal you would like to draw toward you. Surround that objective with the same glowing light. Imagine the person right in front of you, or just let the goal resonate inside. Acknowledge the indwelling light within you.
- If your vision is clouded, what is in your way?

MOVE! *Get Out of Your Own Way*

This is the act of removing resistance (fear) in our minds about taking action. We remove negativity by moving inward, beyond ego: light flushes out the fear. Close your eyes and imagine that you are bathing in a shower of light. The light washes away any resistance you may have about feeling good about yourself.

The difference between success and near-success is confidence.

STEP TWO: The Dancer's Stand
Concentration and Focus

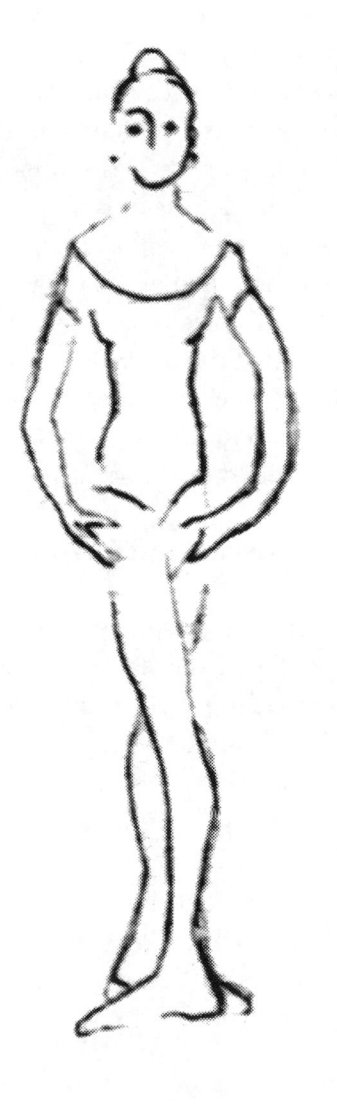

Concentrate, Don't Think!

Ann Pavlova: Concentrate

Rozelle Frey was an eccentric ballet teacher who wore garish hats and black character shoes worn down on the outside of the heels, making her legs bow like a cowboy. One day she said, "Concentrate, don't think!" What did that mean? She had danced with Anna Pavlova, an icon we students could never live up to. Later, as a professional, she came to see me in a performance of a bravura duet I was performing with Fernando Bujones. After the show she commented, "That wasn't it!" Night after night she said the same thing. The last night I executed multiple turns ending in an odd, unexpected move. Then she told me, "That's it, the unexpected! Pavlova had that!" Today I use the unexpected as part of my creative process. Later Miss Frey shared with me that Pavlova was not the purist we'd thought her to be, but was more of a grand entertainer in ballet. And when I danced in the CBC film of Pavlova with Ron Reagan, Jr., she went farther, saying that Pavlova was the Bette Midler of her time. *Really?*

Margot Fonteyn: Focus

On tour in Australia, I was guest-performing in the *Stars of World Ballet*, and Margot Fonteyn—still dancing at age fifty—was also performing. On one of our days off she coached me in a solo from *Le Corsaire*. I thought she'd be impressed with all my technical displays, but instead she said, "You're eyes are static: relax them so your movement will flow. Focus on you, and let your eyes follow your arm." This was almost the opposite of what I was doing. Relaxing my eyes meant I had to calm my mind and focus on my body, which in turn gave me the lyric quality I needed. I had to be more specific with my focus yet relaxed in my mind.

Maya Plisetskaya: Stand Up

Yet another gala tour took me to Europe with yet another legend. Plisetskaya was miffed that my contemporary piece set to rock music not only closed the first act of the show but was also stealing her thunder. So she went to the producers and insisted she close that segment, even though the piece was not a closer. It was only a little thing, but she stood up for herself with clear intent and focus positioning herself where she felt she should be—and rightly so!

Once we understand how to concentrate, we can do something specific within that state of being. When we are specific with our focus we make things happen. Our actions are clear and things flow to us more easily.

Magic is turning fear into belief.

The Dancer's Stand: Concentration and Focus
Awareness, Readiness, Mental Stillness

I learned the essential tool of concentration early in my development. This inherent ability to calm the mind and be present, to focus inward and probe deeper, is infinite. Experiencing the unexpected while performing with Bujones (an American Ballet Theatre star at the time) was yet another step in learning to give way to the moment. I submitted to a deeper experience in that moment by transcending time, and the audience went right along with me. However small or large your desire is, to create something specific requires the quiet freedom inside to see what you want and to entertain all the possibilities. Asking for something for ourselves is often difficult for us. However, when we allow ourselves to be free to feel still inside, we gain strength. To feel that freedom requires expanding inward in order to *feel* stillness. Everything comes from us (our center) and returns to us (our center). Our power lies there—movement in stillness. We can't see the possibilities if our minds are busy. Our thoughts must be still and our minds must be quiet for the imagination to be at play.

To Prepare, to Receive

The best dancers—actually, the best in any field—have the best concentration. Be still and prepare the mind to be ready to receive. When we prepare to receive, we open ourselves to an intuitive message or feeling about something or someone. An idea or image might come into focus, or an answer we've been searching for is illuminated. The dichotomy is that we must be still in mind yet move or take action and focus our intent at the same time. When we are physically present in our bodies through the act of concentration, we are ready to receive.

In the same way, preparing for a test, an interview, or a meeting requires different kinds of preparation. The following exercises are designed to allow you to both experience the state of mental stillness and feel the physicality of focus—making ready to receive and preparing for what's to come.

Visceralizing: Let's Get Physical!
A Standing Meditation

The Dancer's Stand is similar to what dancers do to prepare themselves for daily ballet class. They center themselves within and align their bodies. When we are aligned with our inner intent, it allows our outer actions to flow more easily. Life becomes simple. Even a reinvention of yourself requires alignment.

Exercise

Link to the Dancer's Stand

Stand up: Close your eyes. Be still, listening to your breathing. Imagine your name written across your chest in diamonds shining brightly. Feel an inner excitement about yourself and about something good that is happening to you.

Visceralize: To feel your physical alignment, place your attention on your feet; see them in your mind's eye. Keep your eyes closed while bringing your attention slowly to other parts of your body: your knees, hips, shoulders, head. Place your focus on your own body parts.

Imagine: Imagine that the top of your head is touching the ceiling. In fact, imagine that another head is resting on top of your head as you lengthen up into it and push your feet down into the floor. Imagine that the roots of a tree are pulling the bottoms of your feet into the earth, while at the same time a string of light shoots up through the top of your head...through the ceiling, shooting up into the sky...touching the sun. Feel the center inside of you and directly in front, aligned with your nose. Be still for a couple of breaths. When you open your eyes you will—in that silence—have felt the state of concentration. The next time you stand, while you're in that moment of stillness try bringing a desire into focus.

Coaching Corner: The Next Step
The Physicality of Focus: Three States of Focus

In ballet I teach FOCUS. I break the concept down into three aspects that the individual dancer uses personally. Then we apply the concept to three principals: in training, in choreography, and in performance. In essence, they are inner focus, or placing focus on yourself; outer focus, or placing focus on what you are doing; and projected focus, or placing focus on where you are going.

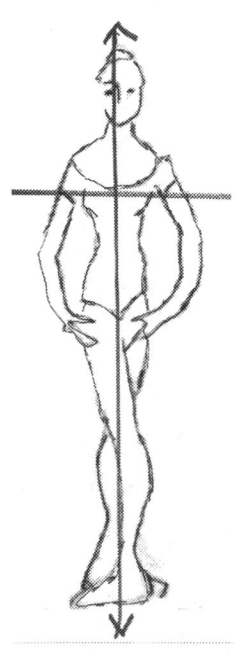

Inner Focus: Repeat the Standing Pose, only this time as you stand feel your intention align with an idea or desire. *I intend alignment.* Feel that you have all the support you need in order to realize this idea or goal. Allow the feeling to be surrounded by light and warmth. This inner intention is the root of the idea that will be born.

Outer Focus: Open your eyes and look at the palm of your hand. Notice the lines. Shift your focus to a nearby object and then back to your hand. Feel this tangible shift of focus. Take a moment to physically feel that a goal you've identified is possible and is actually happening. *What does that feel like?*

Projected Focus: Now look at a window or door on the opposite side of the room. Feel your focus physically shift again. In this moment, *feel* that your goal has also shifted, that it is accomplished. Hold it lightly inside and at the same time see it outside, already achieved. Observe how you feel about having accomplished what you want. Where your intention goes, your dream follows.

Look forward, understand backward.

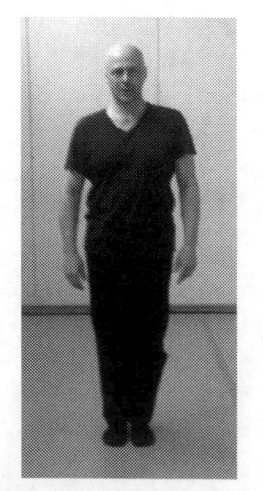

Photo of Steven Speliotis

MOVE! *Get Out of Your Own Way*

Where is your focus? In Step One we experienced magnetizing and bathing in a shower of light. We focused inward on our innermost being. In this step your focus is on feeling your center, your alignment to your intent. Imagine that you're standing on stage facing the audience, and a spotlight is focused right on you. That light not only illuminates your body but also a layer of light that surrounds your body—your aura. You are standing in an egg of light. Feel your aura expanding outward, filling the entire stage with light. The focus is on you. You are moving beyond ego into the essence of you. You are building confidence from the inside out. Enjoy being in the spotlight!

STEP THREE: Plié
Commitment

Just Show Up!

I first met Bette Midler through her choreographer, Toni Basil, when I got permission to use songs she'd sung for my ballet *Midler Medley*. Fast-forward to 2002, and I was giving her private ballet classes at her Upper East Side home in New York City, and she had put a new show on hold. We worked together in a room that held exercise machines and a barre with mirrors. Bette appreciated ballet and approached each class with focus and determination.

She was most interested in a ballerina's carriage, wanting to learn the quality of *aplomb*, as we call it, or radiant confidence, the essential *épaulement*, and various other body "lines" that are formed when a dancer executes classical ballet body positions. She made a strong commitment to dive in and learn basic technique as well, so I began by explaining my dance foundation philosophy, "The 3 Ps": *Plié, Placement, and Positions*. And then I invented a suitable ballet barre for her.

During the teaching process, coaching not just on steps but on other levels often occurs as well. On 9/11 Bette was a bit down on herself, not wanting to make an appearance at some event, and I found myself giving her a kind of pep-talk. The show she'd postponed was *Kiss My Brass*, and she wasn't sure she even wanted to do it. In ballet, when you are distracted by issues or don't feel good about yourself, it's hard to get inside your body to work—and this struggle is easy for a ballet teacher to spot. So I grappled with what to say to a personal idol a major public figure, and then told her, "You know, you are such a positive icon in our culture: it is important for you to just show up, no matter what it is—just show up!" I'm not sure what exactly that meant to her at the time, but the concept of "showing up"— making herself visible—resonated. She walked across the room to a small whiteboard on the wall and with a purple marker wrote, "Just Show Up!" A commitment was made at that moment to be present.

A year later her show opened at Madison Square Garden. There she was, confident yet vulnerable, performing like the brilliant entertainer she is. Backstage afterward, she saw me and with beautiful ballet *aplomb* asked, "So how were my lines?"

Thought can only manifest when grounded in the body.

Plié (to bend): Commitment
Steadfastness, Attack, Affirmative Action

Working with Bette Midler reminded me of what leads to success rather than near-success. She had a moment when she realized the importance of "showing up," and I too had the same realization. I struggle with that issue: teachers always teach what they themselves need to learn! Doubts occur at any level of success—and commitment frees us to move forward.

Tool and Life Skill

Plié is the most important step in ballet. It connects all steps, combinations of steps, and choreography. We all do a version of the *plié*; it is the bend our legs make when we walk or run. Try running to catch a bus without bending your knees: you won't get very far very fast! The *plié* is the "ready" pose in tennis, the shooting pose that gives us the strength to sink the basketball into the hoop, and the batter's pose that allows us to hit the baseball. *Plié* is the impulse of commitment. You must make an authentic commitment before an idea will come into focus. It is the physical state of being that says, "Yes, this gives me purpose. I'll do it. I'll take that step." When you make a *real* commitment to do something, like going back to school, you commit to your goal to continue your education. You step into action and take decisive steps. You act. And with each step forward, you disconnect from your past by expelling negative thoughts that would lead to resistance.

Just do it! Showing up in front of your boss to ask for a raise is easier when we make the commitment to ask. Even doing something for fun, like going to the movies, requires real commitment: we must decide what movie to see and where and when to see it. We take concrete steps. We act. When we resist making a commitment, it is because we are afraid we'll be trapped (by what?) But in truth, commitment liberates us and leads to the experience of confidence.

Visceralizing: Let's Get Physical!
A Flexible Mind

The *plié* is a simple soft bend of the knee. In this exercise, the purpose is to place your attention and feel a focus on your body. This is the first move ballet dancers perform at the barre in daily ballet class. For all humans, it is the first movement in walking.

Exercise

Link to Plié

1. Start with your feet tight together, toes pointing front. Look at your knees and touch them, placing your focus on them. Then slightly bend both knees and place them directly over your toes (illustration below) and in line with your toes. Keep your knees together as you bend. Your feet are still planted firmly on the ground, toes forward. As you press down, feel your entire self rooted to the ground. As you relax your knees in the bend, relax your mind so as to feel flexibility and suppleness of thought.

2. Repeat the exercise above and feel the *plié* as you bend your knees, and now straighten them and bring a goal into focus. Each time you bend and straighten your knees, feel that goal. Commit to realizing it. *Plié* is the breath in your movement. Breathe as you straighten, release the breath as you bend. Feel your chest expand with each breath and become illuminated—feel those brightly shining diamonds.

Coaching Corner: The Next Step
Be in Action

1. Work with the same goal or identify a new one. List one thing you can authentically commit to. Can you take one action on this commitment?
   - Similarly, commit to completing an unfinished task.

2. An old science class experiment, placing a magnifying glass over dried leaves in the sun, proves that the sun focused through the glass will burn up the leaves. That kind of laser focus is a physical action, one that is highly specific. Will you make a laser-focused commitment to follow through on the action you commit to?

MOVE! *Get Out of Your Own Way*

Where is your focus? You are using both an inner and an outer focus as your body executes the bend in *plié*. Standing or sitting, pause for a moment and close your eyes. Imagine that you are receiving light and energy, breathing in sunlight that floods your mind and your entire body with that light. You feel energized. You are abundant energy. You can do anything you desire. Your heart expands with each breath and radiates healing rays of light outward, as if you were the sun, touching others. Breathe in the warm energizing light until you feel at peace with yourself. You are glowing, you are radiant!

Movement in Stillness

In the stillness of the mind is the creative movement of the soul.

Photo by Juan Jose Ceron curtesy of Ballet de Monterrey, with
Lorena Feijoo and Arial Serrano in *Mademoiselle de Maupin*

STEP FOUR: Relevé
Clarity

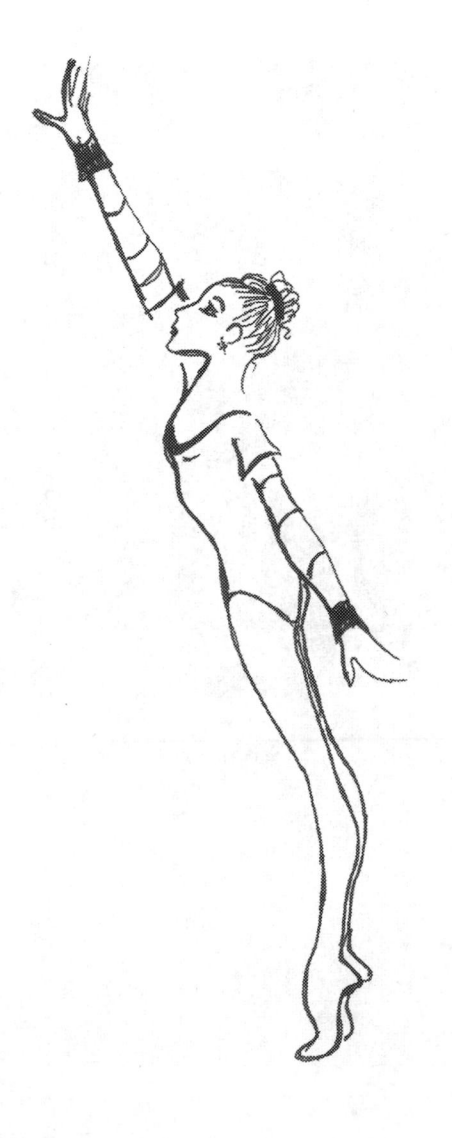

Moving Beyond Limitations

I created *Out of Silence* for the National Ballet of Cuba in 1990. At the end of the rehearsal period, the dancers performed the finale of the piece with unadulterated virtuosity and bravura, spilling their guts out all over the studio floor.. I was so moved that I started to cry. "Are you crying because we were good or bad?" one dancer asked. I couldn't say why at that moment, but what had moved me was a vision of seeing their collective spirits in a unified cry for freedom—for some of them, the freedom to leave their communist country. Months later I returned to prepare the piece for its premiere during one of Alonso's dance festivals, and I was shocked to find that in the interim the work had totally fallen apart. In fact, the dancers seemed to have forgotten most of the piece (a communist attitude of apathy, perhaps).

Instead of getting angry, as many choreographers might have done, I sat them down on the floor and talked to them about personal freedom. I talked about the power each and every one of us has inside to create what we want, not just in ballet but in our lives. I spoke of the power of positive thinking and how, if you imagine something inside, you can make it become a reality. I told them that the ballet I'd created was my gift to them, and that I didn't care if they performed it or not—that choice was up to all of them. "Think about it." I said, "You can choose to do it or not. Let me know tomorrow." I gave them the option to choose—an option they did not usually have. Silence.

As I was leaving, one dancer approached me and said that no one had ever talked to them like that, and it made him scared. I pondered that: the notion of not having the personal freedom to imagine beyond the materially obvious. The next day the dancers decided to perform the piece. Two years later, all 21 dancers landed jobs in other countries outside of Cuba. Several I took with me to Mexico and to the Joffrey. I later learned that I had been a flashlight in the dark for them. Many are still working here in the U.S. and in other countries today.

Alicia Alonso:

Their leader, legendary ballerina and artistic director of the company, learned to rise above a tragic accident early in her career, an accident that resulted in detached retinas and sight loss. She lay awake in bed for months, eyes bandaged, learning choreography with her fingers. Her passion and acute inner focus guided her through the trauma. Shifting her focus to what she wanted to do when she got better helped her to stay positive. Her inner vision was clear, reminding me of a ballet I created for her about the mythical unicorn. The unicorn symbolizes a return to a place of innocence within, and the renewal that comes with clarity.

Shift the focus from "I can't" to "I can!"

Relevé (to rise): Clarity
Elevated Spirit, Perspective

From the *Out of Silence* experience, I discovered that these brilliant dancers were afraid to imagine something for themselves beyond what they were told. They were introduced to the possibility that they could shift their focus to themselves as individuals, not just as dancers, and create different circumstances. With the clear new vision that had been awakened in me, speaking openly with them cleared the air and a constructive rehearsal process followed.

The studio is a sacred space where ideas are born and nurtured. It's just like the sacred place you create within for meditation. The mind needs to be open and clear in order to receive creative ideas or any intuitive information from the unknown. From Alicia Alonso I learned the importance of inner personal clarity. From the Cubans I learned how to transmute that lesson into vision. Today I continue to learn how important being clear is in all areas of my life.

Tool and Life Skill

Relevé is the physical act of rising up onto *demi-pointe* (half-point), but it is also a step where the dancer experiences an energetic lift through the center of their body. The physical move is not unlike what you do when rise up to get a cup out of the cupboard. The lift is part of what creates a dancer's *aplomb*—the elegant way ballet dancers carry themselves, poised and aware, embodying a strength of purpose and confidence. When dancers experience this energetic lift, they become clear about each action that follows. They must rise above negative feelings in order to acquire and enact the varied physical sensations of movement. The metaphor rings true when life asks us to rise above a challenging situation in order to accomplish a goal.

When we argue with a partner, friend, or work associate, we are drawn further apart. If we are able to rise above the cause of disagreement and go to the solution, we can see that the drama stops action as well as interaction. By rising above it and placing our focus on a resolution, we move into something positive, constructive. What is forgiveness but assuming the attitude of *it never happened?*

When we stay clear on the outcome we want, we move forward with greater ease. Be clear. Clarity is the secret to pulling the vision down into the body, and then into the world, in order to actualize it.

Leave your garbage outside the door—then come in!

Visceralizing: Let's Get Physical!
Elevate Your Thoughts

Exercise

Try this move, actually rising up to get a book off a shelf or something out of a closet or cupboard. But as you do so, be conscious of what your body is actually doing, be aware of yourself taking the action.

1. Look up at the object, placing your focus on it. Then close your eyes and get an image of the object inside of you. Open them and rise up your demi-pointe to reach for it. Rise up feeling like you are a puppet being pulled by a string from the top of your head. Feel your whole body being lifted off the floor, almost as though it's suspended in space. Do this again with eyes closed, feeling the image resonate inside and the quality of the life embodied in this movement.

2. Be aware of your toes as you feel an inner suspension in your body. As in the Dancer's Stand, an energetic lift from within now radiates out through the top of your head, touching the sky. Feel an inner suspension as your fears fall away. You are above it all, with no worries.

Coaching Corner: The Next Step
Be in Action

1. A holy or sacred space can be a memory of some place or time that made you feel good, safe. Sit in a comfortable spot, close your eyes, and imagine that place visually or just how it feels there. Feel a sense of excitement and expectancy in this place where no one else can enter. Clear all thoughts and be present in the space. When you open your eyes, think of one thing you can do today that involves clearing. Perhaps clean a closet, or throw away something you don't need.

2. See yourself on top of a mountain looking down at a challenging situation. Feel free from difficulty. From this perspective, rise above any negativity or limitation that may surround the situation. See the solution, not the drama. When you are able to conquer doubt and elevate your thoughts, you clear the way to experience a new perspective. Write down any new possibilities you see.

Move! *Get Out of Your Own Way*

Where is your focus? In this step we are using our inner focus and our projected focus to see beyond our current situation. Close your eyes and imagine that it's a beautiful sunny day and all of a sudden you find yourself standing in the midst of a heavy thunderstorm. The wind is blowing and the rain is strong, trees are swaying. You don't even have an umbrella. Yet you stand there steadfast (like a rock-solid building) in your center, unmoved and untouched by the storm. Soon the storm subsides and you feel a stillness inside. Calm. Slowly the sun begins to shine again, illuminating your entire body. The warm rays of the sun feel good on your body. What does that *feel* like? Focus on that. *I see clearly my perfect plan....*

Stretch Beyond

Photo: Mr. Wiggles

STEP FIVE: Tendu
Connection

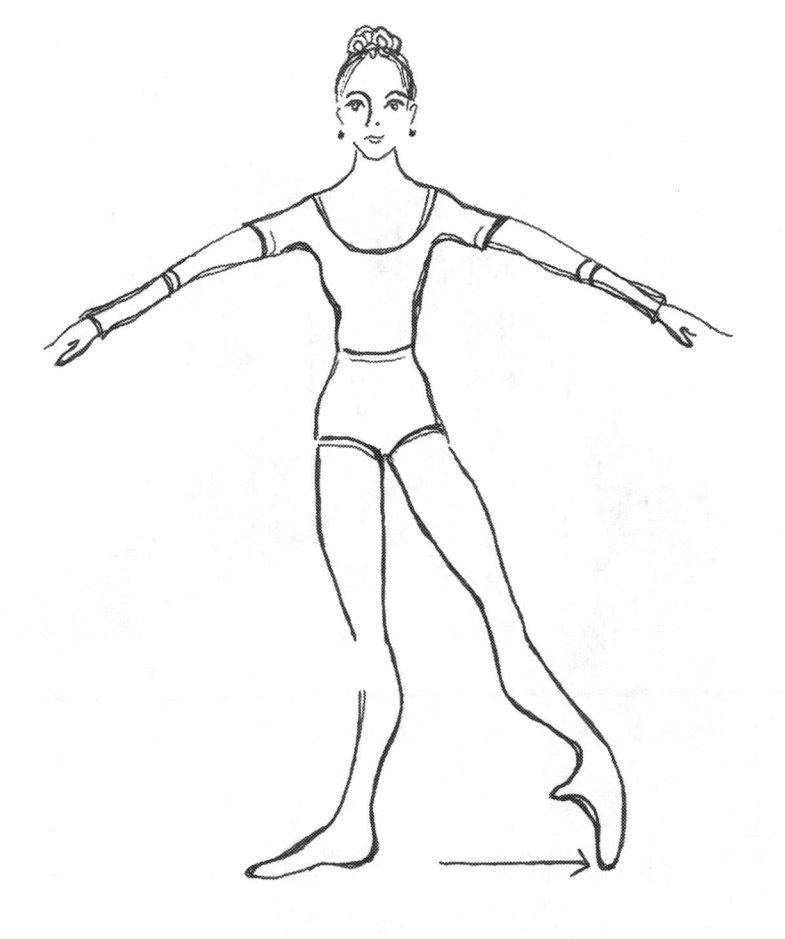

Daysziz Weapons!

In 1989 I was at my first rehearsal for a spot on Sesame Street, with choreographer Toni Basil and street dancer Skeeter Rabbit. Skeet had been part of a Los Angeles gang. Although I had worked with Fable a few years before integrating him into the ballet vernacular, working with Skeet brought different unknown elements. For the duet, I taught him acrobatic partnering moves that only skilled dancers performed—moves he had never seen or done before. It was amazing how quickly he learned. He had never seen a pair of *pointe* shoes before,

either. When I jumped toward him (photo)—one leg bent and tucked under, the other pointing outward—Skeet threw his arms up in surrender and backed up, shouting, "Wait a minute, daysziz weapons!" The *laser*-focused energy coming out of the tip of my pointe shoes startled him and he felt attacked. I hadn't realized that the intensity of my focus—passing through the point of my toe—would be felt so strongly. When he realized they were just shoes, not a weapon, we were able to get on with the rest of the rehearsal. He was forced to stretch beyond his comfort zone, along with me, in order to create together.

Mr. Wiggles: So What Happens Now?

Fast-forward to 1991, when Mr. Wiggles stretched beyond his comfort zone working with ballet dancers in Mexico. It was the day before the premiere of *Paradise,* and I encountered an unknown. Rehearsal was finished and everyone left except Mr. Wiggles. I found him sitting on the floor in the men's bathroom, terribly upset. He had just gotten a call from New York informing him that a friend had been shot and killed in the Bronx. Wiggles was part of the "revolution" in the ghetto for Peace—the impetus behind what is known today as hip-hop. He was shocked, and I wasn't sure what to say or do. So I just sat down right next to him and started talking to him about things—dance, art, artists, the performing arts—and the choices we make as artists to achieve a higher vision. I babbled on about the special bond we have with each other as performers and our commitment to the public. Our purpose to move, to share, to inspire, to entertain an audience was about a larger love being shared—the joy of life. And lastly, what was meant by the phrase, "The show must go on." I gave him the option to go back to New York if he wanted, secretly hoping he wouldn't or I'd be stuck without anyone to replace his unique role. But he was able to see beyond that tragic moment to how his own future as a professional might one day unfold. Thankfully, he chose to stay and the show did go on. We dedicated the performances to his friend, and have worked together ever since. Today he calls me "mentor." My process he calls intuitive: *She writes it as she goes along.*

Tendu (to stretch): Connection
Wonder, Believe, Expect

At the time, putting ballet together with street dance was innovative, scary even, and there were lots of unknowns. We all reached beyond our different dance backgrounds, stretching to allow something new to emerge. That required trust and respect. We connected on common ground through the dance, despite our various cultural differences and dance approaches.

Tool and Life Skill

Tendu is the dancer's pointed foot, which shapes all positions of the leg as well as our lines. It is a stretch that goes beyond the normal use of the foot. Dancers put their mind in their feet for each step, and the act of stretching beyond to see the finished move is the success of that move. In the same way, in order for you to fully form your dream in your own mind's eye, you must stretch your imagination beyond the initial image to the end result you want to accomplish. For example, trying something new like a Yoga class, or buying a home for the first time requires us to stretch beyond where we are right now to what we want to be doing or to where we want to be. When we can't see ourselves doing so, our imagination immediately stops. We stop our future. But when we stretch our thinking a bit farther to see ourselves already doing what interests us and getting what we want, then we make the "getting there" easier and more possible.

There is a direct connection between feeling good about yourself and how you feel about your project or goal. You must feel good about the desired outcome, stretching beyond the obvious, in order to trust that it will happen. Small opportunities connect to bigger and bigger ones, one step at a time.

A miracle is the mind's capacity to wonder, to
believe, to expect good to come.

Visceralizing: Let's Get Physical!
Stretching Beyond

Feel your toes: wiggle them before you start. Draw your focus to your own body. The stretch can be done with the feet or the arms.

Exercise

Link to Tendu

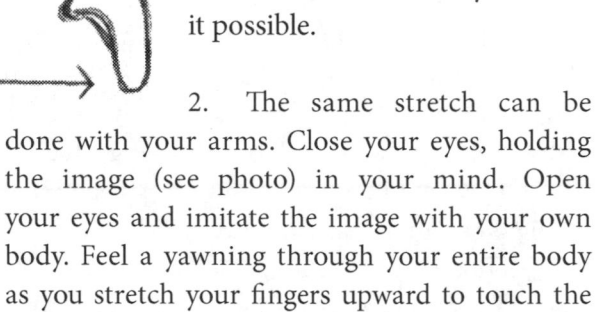

1.   Standing, slide one foot out in front (or to the side) and lift your arch up off the floor to create a pointed foot (see illustration), extending your foot beyond. Close your eyes and feel that move. Then do the move again with eyes open, and feel a goal inside as it stretches beyond the idea toward seeing it possible.

2.   The same stretch can be done with your arms. Close your eyes, holding the image (see photo) in your mind. Open your eyes and imitate the image with your own body. Feel a yawning through your entire body as you stretch your fingers upward to touch the ceiling. Place your focus on your fingertips. Then project your focus up to the ceiling. Feel your focus stretching.

Photo of
Steven Speliotis

Coaching Corner: The Next Step
Be in Action

1. Make a list of people you know and contacts you have. Your connections are your future. What is faith but believing in your actions and knowing that something good will come from them?

2. From that list, choose three people you can contact by phone or e-mail who you feel most comfortable with. Who can bring you closer to your goal? Follow-up is key. Who will make you follow through on this action?

MOVE! *Get Out of Your Own Way*

Where is your focus? Now we are using three aspects of focus. Our inner focus aligns to our center. Our outer focus aligns to our intention. Our projected focus aligns intent to accomplishment. Imagine you are standing on one side of a lake and you look across to the other side. Like a comet of light, project yourself to the opposite side. Feel that you are in both places simultaneously. Light the way for your goal to live in and outside of you at the same time.

See Beyond!

Photo by Herb Migdol, me in Arpino's *Kettentanz*

STEP SIX: Port de Bras
Coordinating a Plan

80 Things...

Conceiving and directing a show the size of Capezio's 125th Anniversary Celebration in 2012—with well over one-hundred performing artists, musicians, visual artists, and aerial artists—required not just organization but an endless amount of coordinating of artistic, management, and production details. That same year I juggled other projects as producer/director for CTFD's *Jump for Joy!*, I was recreating the ballet *Blackberry Winter* at the American Repertory Ballet, and I had multiple teaching jobs, including a semester-long choreography class at Manhattanville College. With several plans already set in motion, I had to plot different timelines for each project. Implementing and following up on the details of a plan is critical for its success—the follow-up being the most challenging aspect of the process. Below is a snapshot of one week out of my year spent coordinating details and logistics and always encountering the unexpected.

To Do:

Artistic meets for show-flow, program outline, script w/Cynthia and DJ Shoe Thread and text. (2) Lisa 9 a.m. (Mon. Wed. Fri.) producing list: Marketing; CapAward; Props from NJ factory for Cobbler Rap; call to Shannon for Nigel; CC rental @ $62,000; Sunday @ $70,000 plus $5,000 rental; $64,000 for Sat. + rental. (3) Almost all dance talent secured. (4) MOMIX request hotel/travel, need load in Ski's in morning? (5) Gil and kids with Mandy Moore need confirm. (5) Program 90 min with 3 different versions - decide. (6) Aerialists need $100 a week for training. (7). Rockettes made several demands + want to open show (so does Tommy). (8). Lombards meet at Ripley Grier: 3 min. of M. Jackson number edit from 8 min. (9) Meet w/rigger Philippe at CC and prod head Mark w/Anna & Emily—Hoop team—rigging/hanging good! (10) Review prod costs w/Mark/Meghan—no FOH. (11) Elka (pregnant) met @ Starbucks, set meet w/Wigz and Crew; Jason on hold if Savion performs. (12) Spoke to Daniel U from NYCB about doing duet w/Nicole (Ballerina & the Cobbler who makes her shoes—in love w/her etc.)—need to coordinate schedules. (13) Nicole needs $300 to change ticket 1 day early from ABT tour. (14) Dax for logistics, i.e. airfares; confirm hotel bookings w/Capezio credit card; music rights clearance; locking in contract with Team ILuminate/production needs (Miral suggests another piece, not Lady Gaga one). (15) Show storyboard laid on floor. (16). Spoke to Rob R on Mon. for Dance Sport Ballroom participants (Riccardo/Yulia too expensive); loved link—a cabaret number to Aretha's "Baby I Love You," but note his couple (note to use on CTFD gala). (17). Tommy T 1/19 for number w/Rockettes; meet at his place 1/26 + need footage of him for film. (18) Meet my film/docu-maker JoAnn (just finished docu on Oscar Hammerstein II)—about 5 min. Capezio docu history/current—her daughter Laura will edit it. (19) Spoke to Ellen Sorrin permission Balanchine Trust—Tchaikovsky "Pas de Deux" for Misty Copeland/Jared (ABT). (20) 1/19 for ILum new deal. (21) Desmond perform a verse from "Breaking in a New Pair of Shoes" (confirm). (22) Ben to do DP press release. (23) KPM PR needs info from me. (24) Martine VH got studio space at ABT to rehearse. (25) More space rental: CC 4/16 week but only 7-9 p.m.; 5 hours each 21st/22nd; DANY Studios 3–5 & 6–8 as well. Costs: DANY is $10 hr. for nonprofit; same New 42nd St.; but City Center is $37.50 less than Ailey or Ripley Grier. (26) Elka to see Capoeira perf/meet w/Wiggles on Sat. at 3:30 after his WRECK session. (27) Lisa signed the contract for the Alex Hotel (need list); 4 for ILum; 1 Wigz and

1 David; 3 for Rasta for 1 night, and 1 for Momix for 1 night. (28) DanceMag is desperate for info. (29) E-mail Nina and list of questions Gil—what piece; 80 from schools plus Travis Wall; 7 piece band "Last Dance" + Abby/Dance Moms; rehearsal time/space? not open show. (30) Phone meet with Lisa /CFO Harry. (31) Meet w/MD Jim, composing new piece "Spinning into Light." (32) Percussionist/ composer Marty away with They Might Be Giants from 1/13–2/24 but on board for composing/ playing "Shoes" piece. (33) Work w/Martine & Hoop. (34) Igal/Yarden showcase see. (35) Dax dancers for Shoe segment (one might go on tour with Follies). (36) Ann Reinking good to present or Brooke Shields. (37) Sent PSM Lori, Brad—lighting & Jim program order and production needs for meet Tues. at ABT at 2:30. (39) Tony W talking Taps w/Cartier and others need Para (need Jaimee shoe specifics). (40) Sent DJ new script/draft. (41) Lisa i.e. need B-roll for JoAnn; Logos Break-the-Floor; Pulse; YAGB; NY Dance Alliance; Peridance-Capezio. (42) Worked ABT w/Craig & Nicole; Met Allegria & Bounce @ DANY. (43) Nina/Gil set phone meet—finally. (44) Dax logistics; plus studio time for Cobbler Rap. (45) Gave Wigz edited link from "Ghettomade" (show Rock Steady Crew guys). (46) Nigel Lythgoe good to go. (47) Ballroom couple to do Liza M song "City Lights." (48) Russ who is on subway—OK to do edited tango (I need the video!). (49) I will use "Once" for Ballerina & Cobbler duet. (50) Rasta suggests shorter 3 min. piece vs. 6 min. (51) Lombard Twins OK for original fee. (52) Wrote "From the Directors Corner." (53) Ben to edit. (54) Peter from Tommy office needs change date. (55) CTFD gala "Jump for Joy" planning to have cast lined up with Nate Cooper, Hubbard St., Suzanne Farrell group, Daniel Cyr from Big Apple, Pucci Sport plus more; Liza Minnelli, Rolex Award (Chita presents); **coordinate** act's needs; Eric for visual projections. (56) Meet about film concept and script + spoke Jose Carreno in Cuba on would perform. (57) Production meet/Brad suggests LED screens @ $26,000 package/$5,000 for the lights/extra crew. (58) Confer with David & Eric (bed at 9 p.m. but up 1 a.m. worked thru a.m.). (59) Rehearsals all day. (60) Meet w/Kevin McA and Lisa for marketing/press releases. (61) Skype with Eric at 5:30 p.m. (he's in Berlin); spoke w/Max in Russia—Arthur Murray dancer on CTFD gala. (62) New budgets w/Lisa—Save the Date on site. (63) Katie review: program issues/payment issues; all W-9s. (64) Misty/Jared fee. (65) Theatre Authority ask/Andrey. (66) Angela Lansbury to host "Jump for Joy." (67) Spoke to Lori K/Rosie's Theatre Kids (Rosie O'Donnell perform with?) for 2013. (68) Shannon/ask letter to Katie Holmes (follow up). (69) Cap gives DR $600 toward scholarship fund—OK it. (70) Speak w/Steven photos/video. (71) Hybrid Mvmt. Co. rigging CTFD call Philippe. (72) Daniel U sends schedule, set rehearsals. (73) Noah Racey "class act" duet. (74) Airfares cheap LA flights now. (75) Finished Directors Corner with photos. (76) Clear song rights Warner Chappel. (77). Cheerleader/World Cup All Stars—OK. (78) Ideas for "Broadway & Beyond" 2013 (Ann-Margret Award). (79) Orfeh to sing Robbins piece 2012. (80) Created new form of work: choreography by e-mail; visit Manhattanville College to audition cast; visit Princeton to audition dancers; determine what to teach/create—speak to designers; **coordinate** all rehearsal schedules (+ dog walker); *America Dances!* project fund-raising with script and business plan to pitch; opening of Smith Center (NBT meet); Valia Seskaya course; Kaatsbaan master class; UCI guest for next year; National Choreography Initiative consult; updating website…

How do you eat an elephant? One bite at a time...

Port de Bras (carriage of the arms): Coordination
Allowing, Embracing Good, Receiving

As an artistic director I pride myself on having great organizational skills. The vision and end goal propels all actions, and the process unfolds organically. Planning well in advance allows time to manage the unknown, and sticking to a clear plan with deadlines makes it easier to coordinate a vast number of details in multiple areas. But good to know that there will always be unexpected changes! A key tool is placing our focus on one thing at a time, and listening and being respectful to people (people make things happen) while staying focused on the end result. Where you place your focus is essential to harmonious relationships of any kind. My goal is to remain calm, holding loosely to the intent, while seeing the big picture. When we lose the big picture we become short-sighted, and we have more of a tendency to create unnecessary drama or get caught up in the drama, not the purpose.

99% of all failure is due to lack of organization.

Tool and Life Skill

Port de bras means how a dancer uses their arms as part of a total body movement. The arms are supported by the back. For a step to work successfully both arms and legs must work together. We call that process *coordination*. It also is what makes a dancer musical. If a dancer becomes uncoordinated, then the step does not work technically or will look odd. Steps in choreography that are disorganized make for a blur of activity or even chaos. Dancers are often given the suggestion *take yourself with you,* which means the whole body, mind, and soul move together as one. This translates in life to putting your whole self into what you're doing or setting out to produce. When you embrace yourself, embrace the need and put your whole attention on what needs to be done, coordinating any plan becomes less effortful.

Something like organizing a long-needed vacation requires these same tools. The process will still specify varying amounts of things to do, but it will involve determining where and when, coordinating schedules, cost, and other details. Any plan needs to be organized and coordinated in order be successfully achieved.

Visceralizing: Let's Get Physical!
Embrace Yourself

Be it a show or choreography within a show, I always embrace whatever the project entails. Sometimes it's hard to maintain control of a benefit performance because talent usually donates (volunteers) their time. But the beast is always able to be tamed. The process we are involved with, in and of itself, teaches us how to be organized on the inside: and we *must* be organized on the inside as well as on the outside. An organized inner mind is half the battle to achieving real success. Inner organization requires a calm mind and clarity of vision.

Exercise

1. If you are near a mirror, reach your arms out to the side, stretching them out toward each wall. See the image, then close your eyes and feel what that image looks like. Open your eyes and place both arms around yourself and feel the embrace. Close your eyes and embrace yourself.

2. Embrace yourself, feeling good about yourself! Then feel yourself embrace an idea or goal. Be positive about your idea, and hold the feeling of that image inside of you. Embrace your goal mentally and physically.

Coaching Corner: The Next Step
Be in Action

1. Pick a short-term goal. Create a plan of action with timeline, deadlines, and follow-up. Don't get overwhelmed! Just set up a daily to-do list, and a weekly to-do list for the sake of getting clear about your options. Then determine what you can realistically accomplish and take action.

2. Embrace a group venture where everyone is on-board the same ship. Imagine that everything you want is coming to you—and you're waiting with open arms. Feel the support of the people you are working with and for. Arms both give out and take in. Don't overextend yourself; know when to push and when to pull back.

MOVE! *Get Out of Your Own Way*

Where is your focus? Become the eye of the storm by remaining calm, clear, and centered. A juggler performs with great coordination. Close your eyes and imagine a pool of light in the center of your forehead, your third eye. Allow that light to illuminate your mind, shedding light on any challenge you might face. Take a step back, breathe, and place your focus on the solution. Open your arms to all possibilities, embracing the challenges along with the successes.

Positions: Position Yourself

Photo: Ballet de Monterrey, me with Roberto Almaguer in *Paradise*

STEP SEVEN: Positions
Courage

The Phoenix Rises

In 1994, as the Joffrey took a downward spiral into collapse, I saw something different: *the spirit of the Joffrey wants to live.* When I told that to Gerald Arpino, the artistic director, he agreed despite what others predicted. In New York the company was in financial crisis, but there was an opportunity for growth in a new environment. I had worked with the company the previous year in a role with no title, which gave me the flexibility to assess freely. Everyone I knew in New York said not to proceed, but with a focused intention to save the company, I was happy to step onto the Titanic. In the interim, I was on the transition committee and was being paid as an artistic consultant by Bruce Sagan, one of the founding board members.

So when the decision was made to move to Chicago and set up the infrastructure of a new organization, I found myself in an important decision-making position. Some of what I was involved in, aside from board-building, was selecting talent, determining the repertory, figuring out how to artistically maintain the Joffrey standard with fewer dancers (thirty), fewer work weeks (twenty-six), and a substantially lower budget. Grooming new dancers was a part of the process of reinvention. During the transition I even went scouting for a place for the company to rehearse and for administration offices. One critical issue involved the possible merging with Danny Duell's Ballet Chicago, and I was able to be part of that decision. In essence, I was responsible for the artistic organization and for bringing back the company's heart and character—again, being a lighthouse in the darkness.

But the biggest challenge was the fact that the company had not merely made a move, it had experienced an organizational death. No one was really equipped to deal with the emotional trauma that was to follow, artistically or in management. Holding to the past created uncertainty, even anger. And for a while blame became the focus, rather than the *future.* There were moments when Arpino and I would be doing programming, and in the middle of it he'd relive a bad board take-over experience. I remember creating a little box to frame that moment, asking him, "Can we put the anger on hold and come back to it after we finish programming?" My goal was always to place the focus on the future, on where we wanted to be. After almost five years it was time for me to move on, and I leaped before I looked back to New York City with grace and aplomb.

The Phoenix renews youth and clings to visions of the future. Today the Joffrey has its own home and is a thriving company. At times, the universe may ask you to leap before you look, taking a new position that may require courageous living. *It takes courage to live and courage to die.*

Hold on to visions of the future...

Passé Pirouette (to turn): Courage
Staying Power - Holding on - Positioning Yourself

With courage, the Joffrey organization turned things around and repositioned itself to survive. My experience with the company occurred at a critical time in my own life and career, a time when I was having to reevaluate my future both as a transitioning dancer and creator. The new had not yet presented itself. It is at those times that we are the most vulnerable. What I saw during the Joffrey's crisis was that it took only a handful of people who were committed to the company's comeback.

And the gestation period was a delicate one. In fact, gestation is an important step in any change process: the five stages being death, decay, fertilization, gestation, and rebirth. That means that when growing a garden "Don't pull the roots up before they fully sprout." The baby steps we take in rediscovering how to walk in the world—literally or figuratively—need be done with care. It is also during transitional times, when we can't see a future, that we are asked more than ever to trust our own process. Feelings give way to visions of possibility. When we don't have clarity of vision, we need to spend quiet time alone as one way of allowing the ideas or answers to come. Being around supportive people is also key, and even a professional life coach may be useful to support our process.

Tool and Life Skill

Positions move. Ballet consists of a myriad of body positions that move in combination with each other. The *épaulement* is an elegant body position, the *passé* is a position that is a pose in itself; but it is also a position in a *pirouette* move. It is essential that the dancer holds the position in order to successfully turn. Dancers are dancer-instruments as they create positions, and allow feelings to pass through them to make movement. It's a paradox. Molding the dancer-instrument requires the dancer to put their ego aside, which requires courage—which is a sign of a healthy ego.

A life crisis can be a break-up or losing a job. It takes courage to accept what has happened and move on. The critical voice in our heads always stops the action, while the heart encourages it. As we act with courage, we take heart. By allowing ourselves to be instruments for our own creative expression, we can better position ourselves for succeeding in what we want. Hold on to that positive feeling in order to turn a negative into a positive!

> **Instruments:** A pianist plays piano for a ballet class, but dancers must mold their bodies to become instruments before they can be played. We are all instruments of creativity. Who-you-are (that which holds onto intentions) is not the same as what-you-do, which is actualizing those intentions. Your authentic self is changeless, but what you do with who you that self are does undergo changes. In the dance of life, allow creativity to flow through you. By separating our personality from what we is created through us, we can more easily have a hand in what we create.

Viceralizing: Let's Get Physical!
Hold on!

These simple exercises make you aware of what position your body is holding while you're taking action. Building body awareness empowers you.

Exercise

Link to Position

1. Walk to a nearby door and place your hand over the doorknob to turn it. Feel this position. You naturally hold on to that position until the door opens. A simple position you can do that is similar to a ballet *passé* is the "tree pose" in yoga. Or try standing on one leg, lifting the other knee upwards to make an upside-down L shape. For example, that pose is on the video link above. Knee lifted, parallel to the floor. Be aware of what this move feels like. Now feel your goal and hold on to it.

2. Bodies don't lie. How you stand tells us something about you. Standing upright with spine erect says you are confident. Slouching says you are insecure. If our heads are in our iPhones, eventually our bodies will regress to look like a cave-man. Chin up and stand up!

Coaching Corner: The Next Step
Be in Action

1. How can you benefit by changing your perspective or taking a different position? Turning things around requires perspective. Staying-power means holding onto the feeling of how you are positioned.

2. Revisit your initial vision for a goal or action. Both your positive and negative beliefs will become apparent. If you are afraid to confront a situation, turn your hesitation into the feeling that the outcome will be positive, and take action!

    NOTE: Spend one hour today not using the word "I."

MOVE! *Get Out of Your Own Way*

Where is your focus? Imagine that you are an arrow of light, and you are aiming yourself at a target: your goal. Shoot the arrow toward the target, hitting a bullseye right in the center of it. As you do this the room floods with radiant healing light, enveloping you. Your every move is supported. Aim your eye at the target and you will achieve it. Take heart and keep going.

What is your position?

Photo by Richard Termine, Ben Needham-Wood in *I'm Really Dancing*

A Dancer's Secret Weapon

A dancer's position for whatever kind of move they're doing needs to be picture-perfect and specific. They must hold onto their position in order to create movement. The position itself is felt, and it needs to be focused. For any dancer, holding on to a physical sensation takes courage and belief, belief in being able to do the move to begin with. In the same way, holding on to your belief about something you want takes courage. Notice Ben's hand—he is using inner focus to balance in this position, outer focus to create the energy for positioning and balancing his hand, and projected focus to sustain the position.

Hold on to the feeling, your belief, and your position. Defy categorization!

STEP EIGHT: Rehearsal Practice
Consistency

PLIÉ: Inner Focus *(connecting)*
Erik Pederson's focus connects the ball to the basket.

PLACEMENT: Outer Focus *(aligning)*
Viktor Franyo aligns the chair on his head.

POSITION: Projected
Focus *(positioning)*
Francoise Voranger positions herself thru the chair.

The Bell Witch

In 2003 I had the good fortune to create a one-act story ballet for the Nashville Ballet with original music by composer Conni Ellisor. Ah, the luxury of working with a contemporary composer! A choreographer sometimes starts with the music (which for me dictates movement quality) and the ideas that emerge to express it, or else the impetus is a poetic idea, intellectual concept or movement-based. Literal story is not easy in dance, but as long as there is a beginning, middle, and end, a story is created. In this case, we were going for a literal story. Creating the work was a very collaborative process. The story, the music, the costumes, the 3D scenic designs were all being created simultaneously.

The story itself was based on a true American haunting, the most documented ghost story in our history. In fact, she has her own website www.bellwitch.com. The scenic elements involving 3D projections had to be strategically incorporated to add novelty and fun to the storytelling. Consistency was key in our creative communications and uniting the story and music. I'd developed some materials in New York ahead of time, so that when the six-week rehearsal period began some of my vocabulary was ready to be used. Once I chose my cast and worked within our scenario, the story began to unfold.

For the dancer, it is only through the consistency of the rehearsal process, practicing steps and new movements that they can learn the dance language through which the story is told. Ultimately, the overall consistency of working with my team toward a unified vision, and being persistent in that shared vision, enabled the ballet to be a theatrically entertaining presentation.

"…The Bell Witch is a grand entertainment…tells the story of the Bell family with a full use of classical vocabulary. At one point, militia men who break into, well, break-dancing…all put together with a craft that shows character and tells the story…"

—Martha Ullman West, *Dance Magazine*

"…The Bell Witch is a perfect example of the unfettered genius that can be generated when artists get together without the burden of high seriousness weighing them down."

—Kevin Nance, *The Tennessean*

Photo by Marianne Leach, Chrisitine Rennie and Eddie Mukrut, The Nashville Ballet

Rehearsal: Consistency
Continuity, Flow, Mindlessness

It is the responsibility of producers, directors, choreographers, performers, and teachers to bring an out-of-focus world momentarily into focus through their work. That is part of the practice. Though dance is indigenous to all cultures, those who perform professionally need to practice steps in order to both move automatically and look natural. Athletes practice their sport. Actors practice lines for plays. Musicians practice with their instruments. Even training your dog takes practice. And spiritual practice in the quest to manifest takes practice. A wise man once told me, "Talent is doing it over and over again." Drop by drop, water wears away stone. Persist. Refuse to quit. Success is practice. Practice is consistency. Success is consistency.

Coaching Corner: The Next Step
Choreograph Your Life!

A Practical Summary

Combining action steps toward realizing your goal is like combining dance steps together to make choreography. It's achieved by moving at your own pace and taking short- or long-term actions. And they don't have to be done in sequence: is a tool for taking action in general in whatever area it's needed.

STEP ONE: *Bringing Presence to a Goal*
List three goals in three different areas of your life—personal, career, and financial. Magnetize those things so they feel vital and alive inside you. Which one resonates with you, which one do you feel most comfortable taking action on?

STEP TWO: *Concentrate and Focus on You*
I suggest the 3 M's (movement, meditation, and massage) as food for your soul, for gaining inner and outer strength. Why?
   a). Movement: Strengthens your body
   - Join a gym, take a yoga class, a dance class, walk or run. Exercise is good for mental clarity and releases endorphins for positivity.
   b). Meditation: Mental clarity brings vision
   - Physical exercise can bring you to mental stillness. Meditation tapes can be useful, or join a meditation class.
   c). Massage: Body-work keeps energy flowing
   - Prevents injury, removes lactic acid, and allows stuck energy to move. There are so many modalities that are offered to us today. Pick one!

STEP THREE: *Make a Commitment*
Looking at the area of career, expand your scope a bit more. If money was not an issue, what would you do? Is what you are doing your real passion? What one thing can you commit to taking action on in the area of your career?

STEP FOUR: *Be Clear*

Be clear on your priorities. Pick one of your personal goals. How clearly can you see it happening? Are you married or unmarried? Do you have kids? What kinds of activities do you enjoy doing (like movies, sports, opera, vacations, gardening) that can put the focus on fun in your life?

STEP FIVE: *Connect to You - Connect to Your Goal*

Look at a career goal again. Who do you know? Make a list of your connections and commit to connecting with whoever you choose. Now, dream bigger—there is support for what you want to do and people willing to help you get there. *Feel* that someone is fulfilling your need. Do you feel excitement or new energy? Are you willing to at least connect to the possibility?

STEP SIX: *Coordinate a Plan of Action*

Look at the goals you've just set or earlier ones. Make a new plan of action if need be, and give yourself specific deadlines. Follow up on any actions you've taken already. Joining a health club, going back to school, or trying a dance class, for example, all require actions and coordinating those actions. Pick one thing that is immediately doable.

STEP SEVEN: *Have Courage to Keep Going*

Do not take "no" for an answer. When applying for a job or pitching an idea, try to get 25 "no's" as a way to see that the answer "no" has nothing to do with how strong your desire is to succeed. If you need to let go of a goal, it should be your own choice. Change your approach if you don't have the results you want. Hold on and hang in there!

STEP EIGHT: *Be Consistent*

At the start of this process, select someone to whom you can be accountable. It could be a friend or coach who will make sure you are consistent with your actions and follow-up. Make sure they check in on you regularly!

You are growing a new belief in yourself and what you want to accomplish. Make it a game, make it fun. Take what you do seriously—your work, your job—but do not take *yourself* so seriously. Lighten up!

Where your focus goes, your body will follow.

STEP NINE: The Performance and Bow
Confidence and Completion

Photo by Myra Armstrong, Cynthia Gregory in *Swan Lake*

ART: Memorable Moments

Cynthia Gregory, one of America's great ballerinas, is the name most synonymous with *Swan Lake*. Her presence was powerful in its grandeur and elegance. Her confidence was unshakeable. As an artist, her majestic quality and technical mastery was complemented only by her vulnerability. We first met on the *Stars of World Ballet* tour in Australia. Later, when she stepped offstage into her own transition and became the Chairman of the Board of Career Transition for Dancers, she drew me into the organization. Also during that time, I brought her to the Ballet de Monterrey to stage a 70-minute version of *Swan Lake*. The ballet embodied the integrity and essence of the original production, with both message and classicism. But it was a most enchanting fairytale. A *Swan Lake* for our time: or rather, a new time!

I still remember a performance when Cynthia danced with the American Ballet Theater. There is one moment in the second act of *Swan Lake* when the White Swan tells Prince Siegfried her story...how she is really a woman under the spell of the wicked sorcerer Rothbart, who turned her into a swan. Just when the Prince is about to profess his undying love, Rothbart wickedly appears and places her back under his spell. As she is pulled away by his powers—exiting the stage—she becomes possessed again right before our eyes. In that moment, it was as though Cynthia's soul actually left her body: the way she portrayed that transformational moment was chilling. It left an indelible impression on me and many others, including a friend with whom I recently had coffee. We both remembered that moment out of the blue, after seeing it many decades ago.

Unlike a painting or piece of music, dance is ephemeral. Artists in the performing arts live on through those magic moments that are held in the memory of the observers. What does it take to leave an indelible impression? What is it that makes your audition or interview for a job memorable? It is the confidence within your very being that commits to what you are doing, as you are doing it; and there's more. It's your soul that shines through you, that lives beneath the surface of you, deep within you. It is your presence.

Creating You is an Art.

The Performance and Bow: Confidence and Completion
Move! Be in Action

The confidence Cynthia possessed on stage and the radiance she still possesses off stage is at the core of everyone's human nature. It is in our souls, vital and alive. As for the art of performing, my experience gave me confidence that I was able to apply in different areas of my life later on. In fact, it never occurred to me that women had less power than men or were not equal to men—ballerinas certainly were!

Tools and Life Skills

The Dancer's Walk will make you feel a dancer's *aplomb*, that quality of confidence. As you place each foot down on the floor, feel authority and command in your action. Everyone walks! It's the action that takes us where we are going and want to go. In this exercise, have a goal in mind and experience a sense of confidence about it. As you execute this step, you commit to move from point A to point B—from where you are now (one side of the room) to where you are going (the opposite side of the room.) You get closer to your goal with each step. As you move forward, you disconnect from the past and connect to the future.

When In Doubt, Initiate

Moving into action brings results: but there are times when we get bogged down by inaction. We can't do anything. We get stuck—our careers get stuck, our personal lives get stuck, we get stuck in a web of inertia. What should we do when this happens, and we're unable to go forward? Move!

Visceralizing: Let's Get Physical!
The Dancer's Walk

Exercise

Link to the Dancer's Walk

1. Assume the Dancer's Stand from Step One. Imagine the diamonds shining across your chest and spelling out your name. Think the words, *I am confident!* Look at the opposite side of the room and walk there with a normal walk, stepping out with your heel first. Imagine the top of your head skimming the ceiling as you move; be aware of it.

2. Turn around and walk back to the opposite side of the room, but step out with your toe first. This is how a dancer places his or her foot. Also imagine that the tops of your legs stop just below your breastbone, not at your hips, making your legs longer. This takes the pressure off your knees and hips. You become lighter.

3. Close your eyes (with someone watching you) and step forward with your right foot and do the Dancer's Walk again. See each foot in your imagination as you continue to step forward with your right foot, left foot, right foot, left foot. Be mindful of each foot as you place it in front of the other foot. Like a dancer, *put your mind in your feet!*

4. Turn around, eyes open, and walk back—first slowly for a couple of steps, feeling the breath between each step and the awareness of your body. Feel your presence. Feel your radiance. Pause, and then speed up the walk, feeling your energy lift your whole body—like a string that spirals up through the center of your body. Repeat. Try doing this while walking down the street, just for fun! Hold your head high, and remember to commit to the moment with confidence.

Transformation

Confidence is the result of feeling good about yourself, and feeling good about yourself makes you feel good about what you do. When you stay in the moment or maintain an unwavering present focus, you are magnetic. By "being in action," you draw things to you. Things come your way, and the unexpected happens. Why does this happen? Because when you are 100% committed to something, your whole being changes. You resonate with high energy and enthusiasm. Your whole being is transformed. You radiate your commitment to success, and the confidence from that commitment is clear. You also feel good about selling yourself or an idea. You feel your power and others do, too. You become what you aspire to be. You complete the action of what you set out to do, and because of that, you acquire internal and external confidence.

Coaching Corner: The Next Step
Be in Action

1. Revisit your goals in Step Eight, and with confidence describe in detail what you feel as your dream expands and success takes a visible shape.

2. Sell yourself! Be clear about what you are selling; but as with anything, they buy you first. Role play if necessary, but remain focused on the quality of your energy, your excitement, your passion—your committed enthusiasm.

MOVE! *Get Out of Your Own Way*

Stand in the light of your own success. Feel success, radiate success, be success, whatever that means to you! Connecting all the tools in your creative process comes together in this step. You are in the state of **Concentration** and are ready to focus your steps. **Commitment** is a physical state of being that says, "Yes, this gives me purpose." **Clarity** in what you commit to is important to taking decisive action. You have **Coordinated** a plan of action, at least on paper, and are ready to move that plan out into the world. Be **Consistent** in the search, the networking, and the follow-up to reveal more potential **Connections**. Check in to see if your initial plan is working or if adjustments are needed. To have the **Courage** to hold on to what you set in motion, review the success that you've had so far, draw on your **Confidence** to do it, and think about the success that comes with **Completion**. Feeling the possibility of your own success motivates and excites you. It gives you energy, which creates the movement that moves you closer to your goal.

The hand in the hand is yours—you make it happen.

THE BOW
Completion

The Art of Process

The bow is not an afterthought. Dancers bow after ballet class, after variations, at the end of a specific ballet performance, and at end of the entire evening. It's an open "thank you" to the audience. Completion really means "ongoing"—there is no end, just a process going on and on. The quality associated with completion is gratitude. Closure allows us the freedom to move on. A dancer's process doesn't end with a performance, because the next day the dancer is in class and rehearsals begin again. In the field we say, "You're only as good as your last performance." Today, acknowledge all that you have in your life, all you've accomplished. Completion fosters confidence.

Photo by Arne Folkedal, me bowing after *Relativity of Icarus*

TAKE A STEP!

Self-trust is the first secret of success —Ralph Waldo Emerson

Photo: Sculpture by Clet Abraham "The Common Man" at River Arno, Florence

THE NEXT STEP: Glissade
Transition Steps

Photo by Richard Termine, World Cup Allstar Cheerleading

Transition Steps

Glissade means to glide. These smooth transitions are desirable! The in-between times in our lives can bring uncertainty...be it at the end of a performance or project, or a loss. Or simply when it is clear that the time has come to do something else. Transition steps in ballet like the *glissade* or *tombé pas de bourrée* are essential to connecting other steps, they serve as preparations for jumps or turns, and they also link combinations of steps. These *moves* in dance that travel from one foot to the next, promising us that we still are moving through transitions even when it may seem as though our lives have stopped. Poor transitions weaken the outcome of a step.

Photo by Carl McClarty of Jason Samuels Smith,
Courtesy of Divine Rhythm Productions

Welcoming the Unknown

Beginning in my Ballet D'Angelo days right up to the present, I have tended to work with or attract artists in transition. When I was conducting a workshop in 2009 for the *In the Mix!* project, that collection of multi-genre, multi-faceted, and stellar talents were all in between projects. Former Joffrey Ballet dancer Jenny Sandler was working freelance. John Selya, who had moved from ballet to Broadway, had just finished a show. Sara Joel and Kevin Gibbs had just left Cirque du Soleil and were going their different directions with their own modern work. Mr. Wiggles, (who has now earned himself the title of hip-hop legend), had successfully recovered from a knee injury and was teaching workshops around the world. The wiz, Anthony Bryant, had just graduated from Juilliard and was testing the waters (he's now with LA Dance Project). And Jason Samuels Smith from the world of tap was on the brink of his own fame, and was developing his choreography and a company. In a kind of not-a-chorus-line fashion, we explored the individual journeys of each of these diverse dancers and their different fields, and we developed some fascinating collaborative work that was, well...*new*. The important thing to remember about going into the unknown is to drop any expectations that we'll know what will emerge.

These last two stories are part of my transition from speaking with my body to learning to speak with my voice.

Shut up and do it again!

"Shut up and do it again!" I was told as a dancer. Ballet dancers are bred to be obedient, to do whatever the teacher or choreographer asks. After a lifetime of speaking with my body, the art of communicating through words is an ongoing learning. Once, when I had to speak on stage, it took me weeks to figure out what to say in the limited time provided. Walking down 56th Street in New York to the theater, I ran into a friend who asked me how things were going. I told her that the event I was producing was in great shape, but I was having trouble with the speech, that there had to be a better way to express these ideas other than through words. Bingo, it hit me. *Of course, the dance!* That's why I was a dancer! Then I realized that my focus was in the wrong place: instead of it being on limiting words, I needed to shift my focus to the essence of what I wanted to communicate, the energy and the excitement of life, and perform my words with my total self. And so the next day on stage I spoke with a new focus and a confident dancer's aplomb. The speech made the impact I'd hoped for and initiated a new beginning. Afterwards, I received positive feedback from peers and a call from Marvin Hamlisch.

You Know I Wrote *A Chorus Line*

When Marvin called to congratulate me on an exciting evening, I thought it was a prank call because he didn't say "so-and-so gave me your number." After we'd chatted for a bit, I seized the moment and asked him if he would write a new song for my next show. I said, "*A Chorus Line* is a show about dancers trying to get into a show: what about their second act? What happens after a dancer transitions? No matter what a dancer does after, we never really stop being a dancer." *I am a dancer dancing when I'm moving or not—I am a dancer dancing even when I stop.*

Marvin understood dancers, and in 2010 contributed *I'm Really Dancing* with lyrics by Rupert Holmes. He played it "live" on stage with an amazing cast led by Angela Lansbury. It took me months to create the number working in a new vernacular between the singer's and dancer's schedules. I had fun choreographing the dance-break segment with the unconventional pairing of Natalie Enterline (expert baton and dance work) and Ben Needham-Wood (mixing ballet and contemporary dance styles with gymnastics and breakdancing); along with ballet dancers from the ABT Studio Company and World Cup All Stars Cheerleading.

Benefit performances are unpredictable because everyone donates their time. But Marvin was a dream to work with. The ever-gracious Angela Lansbury came to a rehearsal the night before along with Marge Champion, who at age 91 needed to teach Randy Skinner (her partner for that night) her special "leg kick" move. Stalwart Karen Ziemba flew in from Los Angeles from another job, learning her part right before curtain, while Charlotte d'Amboise and Greg Butler improvised a crossover. Desmond Richardson stepped naturally into his part, and my colleague David Warren Gibson performed with Ann Reinking in a duet that kept expanding with risk.

I learned the power of flexibility in new ways and how to not overextend in others. Chita Rivera called my music director the night before concerned about her lyrics, but she agreed to read them on stage. And to let me cue her entrance from the wings, which I did... One, two, three, four, five, six, seven, eight—"Go!" She glided across the stage fully in her power and radiant presence and stood next to Marvin at the piano. All very magical. Sadly, Marvin passed not long after that. It was an honor to have worked with someone so brilliant and who cared so deeply.

We are often vulnerable during transitions, and we may experience a loss of confidence. But the more we stand up, step up, and move, trusting our own power and process, we garner inner strength and new confidence. Small steps make way for larger ones. Transitions can be smooth if we know that bad preparations weaken our approach whereas good ones produce a sound presentation or plan. Always be patient if there are delays or holdups. Patience is active expectation.

The Pointe!

Focus brings confidence. With concentration we discover that focus is physical. With clarity we focus on a positive outcome. With commitment we focus on the end result. With connection we focus beyond our reach. With coordination we focus organizationally both inward and outwardly. With courage we gain strength of focus to achieve our goal. With consistency we persist. With confidence we focus on our power. With completion we focus on new possibility. Focus—and congratulate yourself for a job well done!

Triangle of Focus
Photo by Herb Migdol, me in *Relativity of Icarus*

If you draw a line from the top raised hand to the hand extended forward down to the *pointe* shoe on the ground, you can see the stillness. Inner, outer, and projected focus are all engaged.

Photo by Richard Termine, Anthony Bryant in *In The Mix!*

DANCERISMS: Thirty-One Days of Movement

DAY 1

PLIÉ - To Bend, to Connect

Plié is the dancer's breath. The step represents the ability to have a fluid mind, to be mentally flexible, to pay attention to your innermost self. To seek connections.

MOVE!

- Start your day with a deep breath to quiet your mind before taking any action.
- Demonstrate flexibility: patience is active expectation.
- Connect your idea, dream, wish, circumstance to a successful outcome.
- Make a commitment to you: first of all, deep within yourself.

DAY 2

RELEVÉ - To Rise

Relevé is the ability to rise above a limiting belief. The movement lifts the body higher. From another perspective, you can see unemotionally or objectively and move more easily toward a solution.

MOVE!

- From your heart, feel the energy of love rising up and through the top of your head.
- Detach yourself emotionally from unnecessary stress.
- It's a new day. See another possibility, another view, another way.
- Clear heart, clear eyes, clear mind, clear direction.

DAY 3

TENDU - To Stretch

Tendu starts with the stretch of the foot. The feet always take us forward. The quality of stretching is both physical and mental. When you stretch your imagination, you allow the imagined to become possible.

MOVE!

- Stretch your imagination a bit further to see something you want to make happen being realized.
- Feel that you are living in the situation you imagine.
- What does *feeling* where you want to be, or what you want to have, *feel* like?
- I am open and receptive to my good.

DAY 4

PORT DE BRAS - Carriage of the Arms

Arms and legs working together coordinate the technique of steps and make dance movements harmonious. Arms embrace: support yourself first. Love and connectedness allows you to support your own process and that of others.

MOVE!

- Embrace yourself: you are the best thing in your life!
- Embrace your goal.
- All things are possible to those who believe.
- Live in the possibility today and embrace it.

DAY 5

DÉGAGÉ - To Disengage

As the foot brushes off the floor in a tendu position, it disconnects from the floor and extends farther out into space. Engaging in one activity sometimes requires us to disengage from another.

MOVE!

- Disengage from any negative thoughts about yourself or actions you are about to take.
- Disconnect your mind from limiting thoughts. All it takes to be positive is to feel positive!
- Is there something you need to let go of in order to move forward?
- Hope is seeing, faith is knowing.

DAY 6

EN CROIX - In the Shape of a Cross

One portion of this exercise has the dancer standing on one leg while the other leg moves to the front, side, back, and then to the side again. It moves from the center of the body and back to center. Everything we do in life starts with ourselves and returns to ourselves.

MOVE!

- Be centered. Be clear as you venture toward an objective.
- If you are at a crossroads, stay centered and focused, knowing that the right answer will come.
- You have the power to choose the right action for yourself.
- Clear the way. Divine right action lives in me now.

DAY 7

COUPÉ and PASSÉ

Coupé is a cutting movement where the toe meets ankle. Passé lifts the toe and places it on the knee. In both cases the position is key to the action that follows. Holding on to the pose makes the movement succeed.

MOVE!

- Hold on to the *feeling* of your idea, dream, goal.
- Let go mentally of thoughts that prevent you from taking action.
- Cut the strings attached to a negative outcome.
- I see clearly my perfect plan.

DAY 8

FONDU - To Melt

This move is performed with one leg bending lowering the body on the supporting leg while lifting the other leg. It is a paradox of two actions at once. Melting heart gives way to receptive action.

MOVE!

- Focus inward and relax your heart, letting the action melt away any fears or discontent.
- Dissipate: if a negative attitude or past experience has been frozen in time like a piece of ice, see it melt away.
- All past unpleasant experiences are dissolved. Don't look back!
- I move forward with grace and ease.

DAY 9

ROND DE JAMBE - Circle of the Leg

One leg is straight while the other makes half-circles in the shape of a "D" on the floor: this changes when performed in the air. Hips are our life force, legs move us outward, circles renew us.

MOVE!

- What is circling around you today that need be addressed?
- In what areas of your life have you come full circle? Is there a need for change?
- Moving from your center outward requires trust. Trust your actions and trust that good will come from them.
- What goes around comes around!

DAY 10

BATTEMENT - Beating Action

A thrust-action of the foot and kicking of the leg is executed first at the barre in ballet class. In life, our legs carry us fearlessly forward. We sometimes need a kick to get us started or to get us back in action.

MOVE!

- Have the courage to confront something you've been holding back about. You can beat it!
- Give yourself a kick in the pants to overcome an inertial situation. Take action!
- Push yourself forward. Speak up. Let your voice be heard.
- I am all I can be and more.

DAY 11

BODY POSITIONS - Shapes and Poses That Move

A myriad of individual positions forming steps are held in poses and connect to others. A cohesive holding to the feeling/image of your desire is required in order to achieve that desire.

MOVE!

- Align yourself to your dream with clarity and cohesion.
- How will you position yourself, your idea, your enterprise? What strategy do you have in place?
- *Croisé* is a crossed position. Notice who you cross paths with (there are no accidents in life.)
- My intent is aligned.

DAY 12

ATTITUDE - The Pose of Mercury

A leg pose: standing on one straight leg while the other is lifted and cracked at the knee in a shaped behind (male dog at a fire hydrant.) Assuming an attitude of the possible in your approach makes it possible, and vice versa.

MOVE!

- Approach something today as though it were possible.
- How can you change your attitude today about a person, situation, or project in order to make things flow more easily?
- If you have trouble moving forward with something, check in with how you are *feeling* about it. Feelings are pure. Emotions are reactions to feelings and are fleeting.
- "A merry heart doeth good like a medicine, a broken spirit drieth up the bones."—Proverbs 17:22

DAY 13

DÉVELOPPÉ – Developing

The unfolding of the leg. Development is a natural part of any process, whether it's creating your life or creating a career. Like a well-watered plant that grows toward the sunlight, our endeavors grow and flourish. Careful not to pull up spouts before they are ready, destroying the harvest.

MOVE!

- Is there something developing in your life right now that you did not expect?
- Are you birthing an idea mid-plan, or toward the end of your process? No matter what the stage, imagine that your process is complete.
- Like a tree growing upward, move into the sunlight of your own dream.
- The light shines down on me, making easy my path.

DAY 14

FRAPPÉ - *To Strike*

The ball of the foot strikes the floor and disengages. It is a strong thrust of an action that calls for action. Commit to taking action. Life is a game, but after three strikes (or more) you're still not out!

MOVE!

- What does your gut tell you about something you want, want to do, or want to be done with? Therein lies your strength to choose.
- If at first you don't succeed, you have a choice: quit, or try again!
- At the same time, trying with no result can mean it's time to move on. Check in with your original intent and purpose. How do you feel about your venture? Are you still committed?
- All things are as possible as we believe they are.

DAY 15

ADAGIO - Slow Unfolding Movement

Slow-motion movement. Go at your own pace. As you unfold inward, you touch your inner self, while moving outward with intention. This is the root of manifesting. See from the inside out and evolve.

MOVE!

- What new situations are unfolding for you now?
- What situation needs time to unfold and show results? Be patient. Active expectation means doing by not doing.
- Take care with each step, with each action. Stay focused.
- The doors of the soul open inward.

DAY 16

BALANCÉ - Like a Waltz (but not exactly...)

A balancé is a three-step move: a "down, up, down" motion. There is a rise and fall to the movement, a lilt. Bring joy to each moment of your life, in small or large actions. Life is the dance of your heart.

MOVE!

- Timing is everything. In time, on time, and at the right time!
- Sometimes when you slow down it is easier to be in the right place at the right time. You can see between the spaces where possibility lives.
- Steps have rhythm and so does life. Trust your own process and allow yourself to flow with life's rhythm.
- I act now with the feeling of a lyrical dance. I have all the time in the world.

DAY 17

PIROUETTE - To Turn

A pirouette is a turning step that can be executed in different positions, requiring the dancer to hold on to the sensation of the turn. When we're stuck, we've lost hold of our passion. Turning a standstill into movement calls for going in another direction, taking another angle, or simply seeing another perspective.

MOVE!

- Turn a negative into a positive today!
- If you feel stuck about something—someone irritating you, something you thought was going to happen that didn't, or a project that no one seems to be interested in—turn it around in your favor. Be creative in finding another approach.
- Yoga is finding movement in stillness, but dance moves that stillness in space. How will you turn your dream into reality?
- "Live in the dream fulfilled." — NEVILLE

DAY 18

CHAÎNÉS – Chain

A quick turn done on two feet alternating and progressing forward. One step is linked to the other. Who holds the chain of command in your world? Where are there weak links?

MOVE!

- Like a chain-link bracelet, we are all connected. Who have you not thought about that can take you closer to your goal?
- Change is part of progress. Change is two steps forward and one step back. Setbacks can be blessings in disguise.
- When you see the bigger picture and how we are all connected, it is easy to feel support.
- The universe supports your every move.

DAY 19

ÉCHAPPÉ – Escaped

Moving from fifth position, the legs dart/jump out onto demi-pointe (or pointe) to second position. This is also done as a jump in the air. In life, give yourself options: either the ability to move away or to find out where the exit sign is.

MOVE!

- Find the position that always allows you a way out, the freedom to make a choice.
- In any given situation, you always have the choice to stay or to leave.
- Mentally escape a pressing situation and see a harmonious or resolved one instead.
- Be aware of or notice something different today in your immediate environment.

DAY 20

PAS – Step

Steps connect to make combinations, and to make choreography in different genres. Baby steps lead to bigger steps. When an idea is gestating, it is important to take one step at a time. Life has many steps and many ways to step!

MOVE!

- What steps are you taking today that will bring you closer to your goal?
- What steps have you passed over? What steps might you need to repeat? Do you need to take a step back?
- It might be time reevaluate your plans and take a new step.
- When you see the point of no return, it's time to bake a cake.

DAY 21

ALLEGRO - Faster Tempo

For a dancer to speed up movement, the mind first needs to relax in order to allow faster movement. Slow down to go fast. In other words, skipping over details can waste time.

MOVE!

- Pause today and check in to see how you feel about exactly where you are in a particular area of your life.
- Slow down to feel intuitive messages that might give insight to a situation. Check your impulse to act when you are not fully prepared.
- How does slowing down put you better in control?
- I move inward to the life-giving force within.

DAY 22

CHANGEMENT DE PIED - Changing of Feet in the Air

A jump up in the air while changing the legs from fifth position and landing back down in fifth position. The only control we have in life is choice and to change that choice.

MOVE!

- Change happens whether we like it or not.
- Do you need to change your thought about a situation in order to make it better?
- Today change your approach to a normal routine or ritual. Do something different and see what it feels like.
- I am transformed, my mind is renewed.

DAY 23

GLISSADE - To Glide

Transition steps are essential for a strong technique. Life is one big process whereby a transition is just a step toward another transition. If you stay centered, it is easier to maneuver through the chaos surrounding a transition.

MOVE!

- By placing your focus ahead, a smooth transition is possible.
- When in the middle of your process, know that one stage organically leads to the next.
- Effort and struggle are different. Struggle is inherent in being born, but life can be lived effortlessly and therefore with less struggle.
- Only good comes to me here and now.

DAY 24

CHASSÉ - To Chase

A movement that takes the body forward similar to a skipping gallop movement. In life, chasing an empty dream leads nowhere. Make sure you have your feet on the ground heading toward your pursuits and your hand over your heart.

MOVE!

- Stick to your guns. Don't take no for an answer.
- Are you in an endless chase, or being chased? Stop and look, then move forward.
- Take time to catch up with family and friends.
- People make things happen.

DAY 25

SAUTÉ - To Jump

A rebounding jump like a bouncing ball. Jump into or out of situations that don't have value or serve a purpose. To move beyond a limiting obstacle requires your mind to jump out of that situation and envision a better one.

MOVE!

- Think of one thing that is preventing you from getting to the next stage.
- What hurdles have you encountered that you may need to let go of in order to jump to where you want to be?
- When hovering in space you have an elevated perspective, allowing a lightness to come into play.
- Suspend your disbelief.

DAY 26

ASSEMBLÉ - To Assemble

A traveling jump where one leg meets the other in the air. The act of assembling is important to beginning a venture. Assembling the right creative team, partners, and employees is all part of a successful package.

MOVE!

- How prepared are you to meet a challenge? Are you pulled together? What do you need to pull something together?
- Have you assembled the right package for your pitch?
- Are you prepared to confront someone or a particular situation?
- Have you solicited support with clear intentions? It all starts with you.

DAY 27

SISSONNE - Scissor Step

A jump that slices the air with the legs. In life, take a scissors to your presentation. Be concise. Being clear on what is needed assures that your need will be heard. Cut to the chase.

MOVE!

- If anything, what do you need to cut from the past so you can be free to move forward? A belief? A way of being or doing? An assumption?
- Crisis in Chinese means both danger and opportunity. The danger is that you won't survive, and the opportunity is only realized when the old order completely dies in the chaos.
- Let go of what doesn't work and take a chance.
- As the saying goes, it's not over until it's over.

DAY 28

PAS DE CHAT - Step of the Cat

Both legs are tucked under for this suspended jump in the air, moving smooth as a cat. Feline qualities can give us insight into a situation: cats have the ability to hold back and observe before making their pounce, using their intuition.

MOVE!

- Dancers and animals are intuitive. They both know how to spot and seek higher ground when danger strikes.
- Use your higher mind to view a situation. Be intuitive. Don't think, feel it.
- What unexpected thoughts or ideas can you bring down from above today?
- The alchemy of magic lives in all of us, asking for transformation.

DAY 29

GRAND JETÉ - Large Jump

Legs in a split are suspended in the air as if leaping over a hurdle. It requires the most courage to take a huge leap through the air and land properly. Are you able to see positive results when all the odds are against you?

MOVE!

- Pause right now and make a mental leap toward seeing yourself, feeling yourself, or imagining yourself as successful (in whatever that means to you) in your leap.
- How you land is important to your next move. Think of what you might need to give up in order to risk putting yourself on display.
- Relinquish control. Be free to move.
- Grasping at the wind leaves only a clinched fist.

DAY 30

FOUETTÉ - Whipped Move

The 32 fouettés *were first executed at the end of the Black Swan pas de deux. The ballerina shows off her strength and incomparable power in that sequence. Strength is clarity. Acting is courage. Achieving is confidence.*

MOVE!

- Where is your focus right now? Is there any aspect of your life that needs to be whipped into shape? Your body? Structuring your day? After-work activities? Preparing or implementing a plan?
- You are strong, vital, and alive. Feel your power. Keep hold of it in all actions you take now and in the future.
- United we stand, divided we fall. Seek the support of others should your faith falter.
- The sunlight of the world shines down on me, working through me.

DAY 31

GRAND REVERANCE - The Bow

After ballet class, dancers bow to thank their teacher. Applause comes at the end of a performance to show respect for the performer and audience. The bow symbolizes closure and completion and acknowledges a job well done. Feel grateful.

MOVE!

- Do you take the time to congratulate yourself on completing a task, or make sure to thank someone for a good deed?
- What have you started that you haven't finished? Can you complete it right now? Or perhaps you need to let something go so that you have no more unfinished business?
- List 20 things you are grateful for.
- Be thankful, be grateful, be willing.

Be Yourself!

Where your focus goes, your body follows
Where your thoughts go, your life follows.

Photo by Richard Termine, Francoise Voranger and Viktor
Franyo (Uys du Buisson) in *Last Time I Cry*

EPILOGUE
Ask the Dance Expert

Me: Is classical ballet dead?

DeAngelo: Oh dear, where did that come from? In brief—and I know this has been a recent hot topic—my feelings are that since its beginnings ballet has evolved with the times. And what becomes a classic (that which has longevity) in dance or anything else has nothing to do with what is considered "classical."

Me: Alright, more on that another time. So I understand from your story that no one would hire you because you were short. What kinds of obstacles might young people face today in getting a job in ballet or any other field?

DeAngelo: None, if they approach things positively. That applies to any field, really. In dance, for example, the audition process is personal: we all have our own likes and dislikes. You the dancer (and in any job search) are also auditioning the company: Is it the right place for you? Put yourself out there. Be confident. Ask. Someone you know might know someone who might know someone who can get you closer to where you want to be. I was definitely afraid to ask, not because I didn't want to sound stupid but simply because I didn't know what to ask. I didn't know the right questions.

Teaching: Don't take no for an answer. "No" reversed is "On"—move on, keep going on your journey!

On Choreography

Me: Any new voices?

DeAngelo: Not today. The word "choreographer" is too general, anyway, it's ubiquitous.

Me: Excuse me?

DeAngelo: Here's my take on the different kinds of dance creators:

- Choreographers are creators who have something to say (a distinct voice) and who invent an original movement vocabulary to express it.
- Arrangers are those who arrange steps that are not original; arrangers may or may not have something to say.
- Movement specialists are those who do commercials or movies where there is not much choreographic content. This is not to be confused with movement-based work—a contemporary style I call "fragmented acro-dance deconstructionism."
- Routine experts use routines from dance classes, like a three- to five-minute dance to popular music. And pieces that seemingly interprets the lyrics to a pop/rock/rap song. Robert Joffrey, by the way, was the first to put rock music and dance together. Anyway, these anti-innovative routines are popular in the convention/competition arena or on *So You Think You Can Dance*.
- Lastly, a directographer is like a choreographer who assemble multiple talents and arrange moves that have already been created. They are directing the action not unlike a conductor conducting an orchestra.

Me: Can you actually tell a story through ballet?

DeAngelo: Yes and no. Choreographers write with soul. The stories are not so literal, they're more poetic. But in any genre, as a creator it's important to have your own internal story that can take the audience from one place to another. I was teaching college students at UCI about how choreography needed to have something to say, and one student disagreed with me. My response was remind them that we're in the entertainment field creating for others; and in that sense, I'd be looking to hire someone who actually did have something to say. We're in a post-deconstructionist era today, and it's time to go back to the source, the heart of expression, to stories either reinterpreted or that move forward into the new.

Me: How would you define your ballet work?

DeAngelo: One aspect of my work is what I call the "intuitive story," which means that there's a message that has both a psychological impact and contains some form of wisdom. There is a felt sense that can be understood through the viewer's feelings or interpretation. Again, story need not be literal, especially in dance where there are no words. But it's important for it to have a beginning, middle, and end. Here are a few examples of intuitive stories with the underlying messages they contain that I've used in my works:

- **Blackberry Winter** has a message about faith. The metaphor of a long winter frost that, instead of killing the fruit creates a richer harvest. When survival is threatened, trust a good outcome—get out of your own way. Blackberry Winter

- **Crisis** (danger and opportunity) is a message about choice. The danger is that you don't survive, and opportunity is only realized when the old order completely dies in chaos. This story asks us what needs to be let go of to make room for the new. What will you choose at a crossroads?

Photo curtesy of American Repertory Ballet,
Blackberry Winter

- **The Bell Witch** is about courage in general, and especially the courage to love. In this ghost story, the ghost (or restless soul) needs her voice to be heard—and needs to reunite with a love past/lost. What prevents us from moving forward, either in memory or right now?

- **Guy in the White Shirt** carries a message of "false projection," or attaching to a negative outcome that prevents action. Fear sets in when we project negatively: we quit before we start. Detach from the negative before venturing out.

- **Empty Cup** has a message of renewal. The piece was based on *The Book of Runes* concept of the five stages of change: death (of the past), decay (letting go), fertilization (planting new ideas), gestation (nurturing desire), and rebirth (transformation). Martine Van Hamel starred in this piece as the woman who experienced this inner quest.

Me: It looks like you want to say something else about story or the process.

DeAngelo: 50 times....

Me: 50 times what?

DeAngelo: I just remembered a moment in Hohut, Inner Mongolia, when I was choreographing for the Shanghai Expo and rehearsing Chinese acrobats at their circus school. I caught a glimpse of students practicing and was amazed at how many times an exercise was repeated. Of course in dance we practice over and over again, but nothing like this. The exercise began with a student lying on his stomach on top of the feet of a teacher who was lying flat on a mat with his legs perpendicular to the floor and his feet flexed. The teacher then bent his knees and used his legs and feet to toss the student into the air, where the kid would flip or somersault and then return back to the starting position, a balancing pose on his teacher's feet. This was repeated over 50 times, resting for a second and then repeating again. It almost looked like abuse to an American, but it clearly built strength and ensured performance predictability beyond measure. I know that has nothing to do with story—except that *that* moment embodied everything this book is about. Wish I still had the video...

Fact: Life is one big process—with the same old story you keep telling.

Photo Ballet de Monterrey, Lorena Feijoo and Aerial Serrano

Thought vs. Feeling

Me: Isn't it all really just in our heads?

DeAngelo: Well, it's important to be clear on what IT is. Again, IT is all about perception and perspective. And yes, feeling turns into thought which turns into words to be communicated. The beauty of *art* is that communication is felt and experienced in the unspoken, beyond words.

On Art as Entertainment

Me: So how would you describe the shows you direct and produce for one-night events? You defined them before as "art as entertainment."

DeAngelo: Yes, whether it's assembled or commissioned works, they all carry a message, and the voices go deeper. They have heart and soul. That's what makes something classic and stay alive in the collective artistic psyche. The depth of these works (or excerpts) in conjunction with the artists who perform makes them energetically powerful. When combined with works of a similar nature, an exciting fusion of talent occurs that is experienced as a whole much greater than the sum of its parts. I believe that what I do is a reflection of the future. This concept, whether directed by a single artistic mind, a collective, or a collaboration of talents, will produce new and endless possibilities of expression.

Me: When you are amalgamating different voices and producing these evenings, what does that actually entail?

DeAngelo: Aside from the vision for the themed evening, which always comes first, from an artistic point of view it is much like being an artistic director who is either assembling existing works or commissioning new ones. My job involves selecting talent (performers, celebrities, choreographers, composers, speakers), selecting the works to present, wrangling all the artistic and production needs—from music director to clearing music rights, to hiring extra crew like riggers for an aerial work— to managing the talent and their needs: air tickets, hotels, per diems, studio space rental, costumes, and multifarious other travel needs. Each year I assemble casts of over one-hundred performers. I have a small staff and artistic committee, and also lead my production team: stage manager, lighting designer, music director, script writer, video artists, and more. And I work alongside the CTFD staff, PR and marketing departments, and design team to create the program journal and related things. All in all, I am working closely with about 50 people every year, not counting the actual one-hundred-plus performers.

Me: The bigger the production, the bigger the beast!

DeAngelo: Yes, and I have ways that I can control that the beast. The Capezio 125th show for example, was probably one of the largest shows I've created. Loved the shoe theme: it was a great show thread. The talent and their dance genres told their stories from the perspective of their shoes. One scene involved a dance-shoe cobbler who was in love with the ballerina (see photo) whose shoes he made. And she was absolutely dependent on him to enable her to perform her craft (and this is a true story)! Jac Venza, the public television producer responsible for bringing the arts to PBS, congratulated me on how well the concept and theme worked. Today I am continuing to develop this concept.

Dancers: Nicole Graniero and Craig Salstein

On What's New

Me: So what's new?

DeAngelo: Nothing.

Me: You mentioned new eras be birthed by women?

DeAngelo: Historically that's been the case, at least in dance. For example, look at the founders of the major classical ballet companies: American Ballet Theatre, Lucia Chase; The Royal Ballet, Ninette de Valois; The National Ballet of Canada, Celia Franca; The National Ballet of Cuba, Alicia Alonso; The Australian Ballet, Peggie Van Pragg. And women have been the founders of the most innovative dance: Duncan, Graham, DeMille, Cullberg, Bausch, Tharp. Dance is currently in a period of rebirthing, revisioning, and recreating its purpose—and that process, like birthing, comes from women.

Me: In one word, what's missing today?

DeAngelo: Vision. That unspoken, intuitive quality that sees before others do. Vision creates distinction and character. Dance is now become firmly embedded in the consciousness of our culture, and ballet has proliferated across the country. But at the same time, ballet has lost distinction both in companies and in ballets. A homogeneity of sorts pervades, in a time where being distinct is more sellable.

Me: I don't see much dance, so I wouldn't know. Go on....

DeAngelo: Character is the key to the success of any product we buy or sell. And after all, ballet is synonymous with character: character is the essence of the male and female roles of the classics and in any of the story ballets. Modern companies also take on the character of the choreographer. Character in painting is obvious: look at Picasso versus Andy Warhol, for example. In music, consider Bach versus Copland, or the Beatles versus the rap music of today. Character is vital to the arts and entertainment, and character comes from the artistic vision.

Attitude: Expect! I can because I think I can.

Me: Can you talk more about creative destruction?

DeAngelo: The light-bulb replaced the candle. The car replaced the horse and buggy, and so on. As in any turn-of-the-century period, we are living in a time where new things, new ways of doing things, and new ways of being are being generated. New structures and new models are emerging. What we believe about the way we do things is changing and evolving before our very eyes. Separativeness is now giving way to unity. DeAngelo Productions reflects a new model, a new paradigm, if you will, in which artists collaborate and are hired for skill set or a need, not a job description. We don't really have an office in the traditional sense. We work remotely, yet we're in constant contact and can manage large projects extremely efficiently.

On Transition

Me: What are your thoughts on transition, for people in general?

DeAngelo: For dancers, transition is forced. It is hard to replace the immediate gratification of performing with the routines of daily life; no one applauds you when you make a phone call or go shopping. But for all of us, life is one big transition. If you think of it that way, it's easier to maneuver through the planned or unplanned changes we encounter. Again, the scariest thing for all of us is to not be able to see our future: the unknown.

Me: I see from the list at the end of the book that you've worked with a variety of theater and star personalities in different arenas. In one word or less, tell me something about a few of them. Liza Minnelli?

DeAngelo: Vulnerable.

Me: Bebe Neuwirth?

DeAngelo: Perfectionist.

Me: Angela Lansbury?

DeAngelo: Consistent.

Me: James Earl Jones?

DeAngelo: Poetic.

Me: Bette Midler?

DeAngelo: Wise.

Me: Chita Rivera?

DeAngelo: Sharp.

Me: Maurice Hines?

DeAngelo: Showmanship.

Me: Nigel Lythgoe?

DeAngelo: Calculating.

Me: Brooke Shields?

DeAngelo: Humility.

Me: Rosie O'Donnell?

DeAngelo: Generous.

AMD: Ann Reinking?

DeAngelo: Warmth.

Me: Ann-Margret?

DeAngelo: Ann-Margret!

Me: Paula Abdul?

DeAngelo: Grateful.

Last Thoughts

Me: So what is your book really about?

DeAngelo: Focus. I walk my dogs off-leash in New York City, always have, for over twenty-five years. People always say, "Don't walk your dogs off the leash, idiot. They'll run into the street!" My dogs never have: it's other people's fear, not mine.

Me: Because the dogs are *focused*?

DeAngelo: OK, another story. For thirty years people have also told me to not carry an open dance bag on my shoulder. "Hey, don't leave your dance bag open like that. Someone will steal something!" Never happened. Their fear, not mine. I am not focused on the fear.

Me: If you're not focused on fear, what it is that you focus on?

DeAngelo: I'm walking east on 12th Street in Greenwich Village and a blind lady with her seeing-eye dog is walking toward me. Now, most people think the obvious: "Oh, it's a blind lady and her seeing-eye dog walking toward me." But I think something beyond, something more aware and more profoundly concerned: "Who picks up the poop of that seeing-eye dog?" I am always focused on the solution.

Endorsements

CTFD Gala 2014:
http://www.broadwayworld.com/article/Photo-Flash-Angela-Lansbury-James-Earl-Jones-Chita-Rivera-Michael-Dameski-and-More-at-Career-Transition-For-Dancers-29th-Jubilee-20141008
"The show once again produced and directed by Ann Marie DeAngelo was a 90-minute non-stop, high kickin', electrifying evening that left the audience breathless."

"Ann Marie DeAngelo lives and practices what she's written in this book. She was one of the shortest ballerinas. What could she do about her height to change it? Technically not anything, and yet she flew past barriers, she altered perception, she changed the very definition of what being a ballerina meant with respect to body. How did she do this? Mind over matter. Determination. Discipline. Time and again, DeAngelo has broken through the seemingly impossible, in part by helping others be able to "see" what is possible. She took Gerald Arpino by the hand when his Joffrey Ballet was on the brink of extinction, for example, and showed him how to regain a company of substantial dancers, reposition the repertory, and physically relocate from NYC to Chicago where it thrives today. What's in this story for you? As DeAngelo shows through a multitude of stories, her principles for rising above obstacles can belong to everyone. They apply to small life moments, as well as big. They help you focus and see how to make the impossible possible."
—Sasha Anawalt, Author of "Joffrey: Mavericks of American Dance"

"Ann Marie DeAngelo is one of the brightest and most innovative people working in the dance world today. She was an amazing performer, and is an artist with a deep understanding of human nature and the human body. This book is a gift of ideas and new thoughts for all."
—Cynthia Gregory, American ballerina

"Ann Marie's distinct creativity and brilliant choreography turned our 125th year celebration for Capezio Ballet Maker's Inc. into a grand, total success. The respect from her peers and the industry were obvious. I am grateful to her, as through her art, that made you feel something that resonated within all of us."

—Lisa A. Giacoio Egan, President
Capezio Ballet Maker's Dance Foundation

"Ann Marie DeAngelo has always been ahead of the creative curve. Whether it was as a principal dancer with the Joffrey Ballet or as a director/choreographer of her very successful dance theater pieces "Zeitgiest" I and II and "The Last of the Best" or her current work as director of the Career Transitions For Dancers yearly Gala at City Center in New York. Ann Marie creates works that set trends for others to follow. Anyone interested in where theater art is headed should pay attention to what this artist is doing next."

—Daniel J. Giagni, CEO Distinctive Builders
(Former Broadway choreographer and Tony nominee)

"Ann Marie and I danced together in the Joffrey Ballet. One day on tour when talking to Gerald Arpino, he said to me—in his direct, hard as nails cloaked with love, Staten Island way, 'Jeff baby, if you could get out of your own way, you could fly. You are pals with Ann Marie, just learn her habits of daily commitment and relentless dedication and you will be surprised at what could happen.' As students I remember being struck by the power that emanated from her technique. There was a singularity of focus that created a charisma that was riveting to say the least. But it was obvious that she was better than anyone else, better not only in what she commanded as a technician but just better because of her will. It is a daily technique that Ann Marie employs and a technique that she can teach, if one is receptive and ready to move up and forward. Later when she was the founding artistic director of Ballet de Monterrey (BdM), she as guided by her intuition, invited me to come to BdM to be her associate director/ballet master. She invited me because she had a feeling it would be right—a risk since I had not had that level of a position previously. It is how she operates, she trusts herself and makes decisions that have a basis in realism, but come from an idea that no one else has seen or had. She makes things happen. That is how BdM came into existence, and with Yolanda producing it. Then she took it a step further as a pioneer, where through her, BdM became a conduit for dancers coming out of Cuba into Mexico and then America and

Europe. She was highly instrumental in opening the doors for the fantastic Cuban dancers that are in companies around the world now."

—Jeffrey Graham Hughes, director, choreographer, teacher

"When I needed someone for guidance about the next steps in my career and relating it to my passion in dance, Ann Marie was a great help!"

—Molly Lynch, Artistic Director
National Choreographers Initiative

"Ann Marie DeAngelo has helped me to think big and think beyond. Her expert advice, her keen eye and her collaborative energy has helped me remain continually inspired by possibility, and the dance."

—Tony Waag, Artistic Director
American Tap Dance Foundation

Letter from a Muse

Dearest Friend,

You never cease to amaze me! I've admired you ever since I met you, everything about you: your creativity, your infrared vision for discovering talent of all kinds, your generosity that shares it with the world without expectation of reward, your vision of excellence—knowing and wanting to work with the best—your ingenuity, your capacity to bring together artists and people of all backgrounds and art forms and put them together in the most inexplicable, magical forms to create a show, ballets, stories... When I first met you 24 years ago, I could see that you were way ahead of your time. You were able to produce greatness even in places like Cuba, where no one dared to go. I am forever in awe of what you do and what you are. You are truly a revolutionary and a visionary at heart. Much love to you and congratulations on all your achievements, but especially congratulations for being YOU!

Lorena Feijoo, 2014

Me: I know we're done with this interview, but the last last thing... do you have a list of some of the talents you've worked with and presented?

DeAngelo: Yes, of course, a few...

PRODUCING OTHERS

Companies and Talent

Dance Companies
The Ailey School
Alvin Ailey American Dance Theater
ABT II
American Ballet Theatre
American Repertory Ballet
American Tap Dance Foundation
Atlanta Ballet
Anti-Gravity
Bad Boys of Dance
Balam Dance Theatre
Ballet de Monterrey
Ballet San José Silicon Valley
Ballet Hispanico
Ballet Trockadero
Big Apple Circus
Jonah Bokaer
Break the Floor
Broadway Dance Lab
Bullettrun
Carolina Ballet Theatre
Cedar Lake Contemporary Ballet
Cirque du Soleil
Complexions
Dance Theatre of Harlem
DTH: Dancing Through Barriers Ensemble
Dance Sport Ballroom
Dance Times Square
Pierre DuLaines "Dancing Classrooms"
Dancing Wheels
Dance China NY
David Parsons Dance Company
Decadancetheatre
Donny Golden Irish Dance

Drum Cafe NY

Electric Boogaloos

Industrial Rhythm

Lori Belilove & Isadora Duncan Dance Company

Jennifer Muller/The Works

Arthur Murray Dancers

Jason Samuels Smith and Friends

The Joffrey Ballet

The Houston Ballet

Hybrid Movement Company

Hubbard Street Dance Chicago

Houston Ballet Theater

Industrial Rhythm

Lar Lubovitch Dance Company

The Lombard Twins

iLuminate

Luna Negra Dance Theater

Mark Stuart Dance Theater

Miami City Ballet

MOMIX

Arthur Murray Dancers

Mr. Wiggles and Electric Boogaloos

New York City Ballet

New York Theatre Ballet

National Dance Institute

National Dance Institute of New Mexico

New Jersey Tap Ensemble - Teen Rep

Noah Racey's New York Song & Dance Company

Ohio Ballet

Ologunde

Parallel Exit

River North Chicago Dance

Rosie's Theater Kids

Rock Steady Crew with Crazy Legs

Parul Shah Dance Co.

Peter Pucci Plus Dancers

Pucci Sport

San Francisco Ballet

Sachiyo Ito
Semperoper Ballett
Silva Dance Company
Sonya Tayeh Dance
Sounds of Korea
Suzanne Farrell Ballet
Tap City Youth Ensemble
The Rockettes
The Rockette Alumnae
The Street Beats Group
Thunderbird American Indian Dancers
World Cup Shooting Stars / All Star Cheerleading
Wylliams/Henry Dance Company

Choreography: (A few, past and present, in all genres)

Gerald Arpino, Debbie Allen, George Balanchine, Toni Basil, Michael Bennett, Andy Blankenbuehler, Josh Bergasse, Val Caniparoli, Alejandro Cerrudo, Nate Cooper, Lynne Taylor-Corbett, Danny Daniels, David Dawson, Agnes de Mille, Christopher d'Amboise, Laura Dean, Ann Marie DeAngelo, Isadora Duncan, Mark Stuart Eckstein, Mercedes Ellington, Carlos Fittante, Bob Fosse, Robert Garland, Kevin Gibbs, Christopher Harrison & Mam Smith, Robert Hill, Sara Joel, Alan Johnson, Alonso King, Maxim Kozhevnkiov, Nadia Lesy, Martin & Facundo Lombard, Lar Lubovitch, Tony Meredith & Melanie LaPatin, Molutsi Mogami, Mandy Moore, Charles Moulton, Jennifer Muller, Dennis Nahat, Catherine Oppenheimer & Lori Klinger, David Parsons, Moses Pendleton & Company, Marius Petipa, Benoit-Swan Pouffer, Josh Prince, Peter Pucci, Noah Racey, Ann Reinking, Dwight Rhoden, Jerome Robbins, Pedro Ruiz, Alex Sanchez, Margo Sappington, Randy Skinner, Susan Stroman, Jason Samuels Smith, Tony Stevens & Carol Schuberg, Sonya Tayeh, Twyla Tharp, Francoise Voranger, Tony Waag, Jennifer Weber, William Whitener, Mr. Wiggles, Keith Young, Rostislaz Zakharov

Hosts, Presenters, or Awardees

Paula Abdul, Mikhail Baryshnikov, Laura Benanti, Marge Champion, Charlotte d'Amboise. Jacques d'Amboise, Carmen de Lavallade, Sandy Duncan, Mercedes Ellington. Nicole Fosse, Sutton Foster, Cynthia Gregory, Valerie Harper, Judith Jamison, James Earl Jones, Angela Lansbury, Nigel Lythgoe, Shirley MacLaine, Peter Martins, Kathleen Marshall, Malcolm McDowell, Donna McKechnie, Liza

Minnelli, Brian Stokes Mitchell, Jerry Mitchell, Bebe Neuwirth, Phylicia Rashad, Samuel Ramey, Ann Reinking, Chita Rivera, Brooke Shields, Ben Vereen, Edward Villela, Karen Ziemba

Some Featured Performers

Kelly Bishop, Ashley Bouder, Sandra Brown, Anthony Bryant, Andy Blankenbuehler, Jose Emanuel Carreño, Mary Carmen Catoya, Will Chase, Lynn Cohen, Nate Cooper, Misty Copeland, Herman Cornejo, Daniel Cyr, Crazy Legs, Charlotte d'Amboise, Michael Dameski, Kent Drake, Preston Dugger, Sandy Duncan, Mercedes Ellington, Natalie Enterline, Lorena Feijoo, Mary Verdi-Fletcher, Miguel Frasconi, Marilyn Taylor Gleason, Marcelo Gomes, Kevin Gibbs. David Warren Gibson, Nicole Graniero, David Hallberg, Paloma Herrera, Marvn Hamlisch, Dule Hill, Blaine Hoven, Jazzy J, Cheyenne Jackson, Tai Jimenez, Sara Joel, William Johnston, Julianne Kepley, Jason Kittelberger, Maria Kowroski, Jane Krakowski, Melody Lacayanga, LaChanze, Robert LaFosse, Mary Ann Lamb, Angela Lansbury, Jane Lanier, Melanie LaPatin, Eric Lewis, Shannon Lewis, The Lombard Twins, Lypsinka, Mary Macleod, Andrea McArdle, Tony Meredith, Abby Miller (Dance Moms), Dana Moore. Mouse, Richard Move, Bebe Neuwirth, Christian Noll, Rosie O'Donnell, Orfeh, Elizabeth Parkinson, Veronika Part, Peter Pucci, Billy Porter, Noah Racey, Ann Reinking, Xiomara Reyes, Desmond Richardson, Chita Rivera, Keith Roberts, Raymond Rodriguez, Daniil Simkin, Jason Samuels Smith, Gennadi Saveliev, Acacia Schachte, Benji Schwimmer, John Selya, Willy Shives, Pam Sousa, Isaac Stappas, Melinda Sullivan, Stretch, Jimmy Tate, Rasta Thomas, Tommy Tune, Vanessa Valecillos, Anna and Emily Venizelos, Andrew Veyette, Travis Wall, Mr. Wiggles, Michele Wiles, Maia Wilkins, Cartier Williams, Donald Williams, Karen Ziemba

Credits and Thank You's!

A BIG THANK YOU to Cynthia Gregory for your artwork, Barbara Goodman Springer for encouragement, editor Madeleine Fahrenwald and Charmaine Wakefield for support, proofing, and editing. And to those who were not encouraging—all input is good.

Photos: Cover and back photo by Herb Migdol (and others) are of me. Thank you, Herb! And thank you Arne, and thank you Richard!

Wow!

Photo by Richard Termine, Kevin Baron mid-air, me, and Viktor in the back

About the Author

Ann Marie DeAngelo is an expert in all types of dance. The former Joffrey Ballet principal dancer was featured in TIME Magazine as one of America's most outstanding ballerinas, later becoming the associate director of the Joffrey. She was artistic director of Ballet D'Angelo, an experimental troupe touring extensively in Europe, followed by serving as the founding artistic director of Ballet de Monterrey, the first privately funded arts organization in Mexico. DeAngelo has choreographed over 60 ballets and a new musical in China for the Shanghai Expo 2010. Her one-act ghost story The Bell Witch was nominated for the prestigious Benois de la Danse Award, and a segment was performed at the Bolshoi Theater in Moscow.

As producer/director of the annual Career Transition For Dancers Gala benefit at City Center in New York, she has created twelve dance evenings. In them she has presented hundreds of artists and dance companies and has worked with personalities that include: Paula Abdul, Marge Champion, Dule Hill, Sutton Foster, Marvin Hamlisch, James Earl Jones, Jane Krakowski, Angela Lansbury, Nigel Lythgoe, Ann-Margret, Liza Minnelli, Bebe Neuwirth, Rosie O'Donnell, Ann Reinking, Chita Rivera, Brooke Shields, Tommy Tune, and Ben Vereen. DeAngelo Productions is the producing entity for the variety dance-extravaganzas she is known for, including Capezio's 125th Anniversary show.

She has worked as an artistic consultant for several arts organizations, taught in numerous ballet and contemporary dance companies, universities, and summer courses, and has been movement coach to Bette Midler. Her program Bringing Performance to Life was initiated at Rancho La Puerta. DeAngelo lives in New York City.

Printed in the United States
By Bookmasters